KEY TO FIRST ENGLISH GRAMMAR

KEY TO FIRST ENGLISH GRAMMAR

ALEXANDER BAIN

GYAN

Published by

GYAN

Gyan Publishing House
5, Ansari Road
Daryaganj, New Delhi-110002
Phone: 011-47034999, 9811692060
E-mail: books@gyanbooks.com

Distribution Network
gyanbooks.com
India, USA, Canada, UK, Australia

ISBN: 978-93-7414-104-5 (PB)

First Published, 1872

2nd Impression 2026

Printed at: Gyan Press, Delhi.

KEY TO FIRST ENGLISH GRAMMAR
Author: ALEXANDER BAIN

KEY

TO

FIRST ENGLISH GRAMMAR

BY

ALEXANDER BAIN, LL.D.,

PROFESSOR OF LOGIC IN THE UNIVERSITY OF ABERDEEN.

LONDON: LONGMANS AND CO.

1872.

ABERDEEN:
PRINTED BY ARTHUR KING AND COMPANY, PRINTERS AND STEREOTYPERS
CLARK'S COURT, TOP OF BROAD STREET.

PREPARATORY EXPLANATIONS.

Answers to Questions (p. 27).

THESE questions extend over the whole of the Preparatory Explanations. They are taken up in order; and the **Exercises** (**1, 2, 3**) are noticed in the place that they occupy in the succession of the Questions.

Q. 1-7. SPEECH OR DISCOURSE.

In this section the teacher's chief care should be to impress upon the pupils, by every variety of statement and illustration, the two cardinal functions of words.

It will not do to say simply that one class of words *name* or *point out* persons, things, actions, &c.; and that the other class *tell or declare something about* them. The great distinction between *naming* and *declaring* may be explained as follows:—

When I simply say 'John Thomson,' or 'The Americans,' or 'The Jews of Amsterdam,' I merely point out who I am going to speak about. If I stop after having said 'The Americans,' or 'The Jews of Amsterdam,' the person that I address says—'Well, what about them?' These words merely show the subject of my discourse. One great purpose of words, then, is to show what I mean to speak about.

On the other hand, if I say—'is in the garden,' or—'are rapidly increasing in numbers,' or—'are very greedy,' any person hearing me would ask—'Who are you speaking about? Who is the subject of your remarks? You have made a declaration; who do you make it about?'

In some such way as this the teacher may bring home to his pupils the distinction between naming on the one hand, and telling, declaring, or affirming on the other. He will choose familiar examples, and give 'naming' expressions and 'declaring' expressions separately, so as to impress upon the mind that the one sort of words are useless without the other. There will be no harm although he anticipate a little the order of the grammar; and explain at once that the first class are called Subjects, and the second Predicates. He may then ask one pupil to give a subject, and another to give a predicate to it; one to name some subject of knowledge, and another to make a declaration about it, and so forth; using every artifice to make the pupils think, and not merely repeat.

When the teacher comes to the list of subjects of knowledge, where he has to exercise the pupils by such questions as No. 6, he may propound such puzzles as—'Name an action, and tell me something about it:' 'Name an animal, and make a declaration about it.' He may then repeat the words of the subject or of the predicate, and ask what use or function they serve, and what designations are given to them.

Q. 8-25. SUBJECTS OR THINGS SPOKEN OF.

It might be rather confusing if the pupil were asked to do nothing more than go over the examples in the text, and repeat that the things named agree, or differ, as the case may be. The striking point for the young mind is that we know nothing else about things than that they differ and agree; all our knowledge about a thing may in the last resort be resolved into differences and agreements with other things. This should be stated in connection with Q. 8, and brought home as far as possible, not only in the examples given, but also by reference to objects immediately under the pupil's eye.

Q. 9 involves a point somewhat difficult to grasp: namely, that 'up' has no meaning except as the opposite of 'down,' 'long' no meaning except by comparison with 'short.' A man that appears tall to a child would appear short to a giant: a porter strong by comparison with a slender stripling, is weak by comparison with Samson; a man with £300 a-year is considered poor by a man with £3000 a-year.

Q. 10 should be illustrated practically.

Q. 11. Among the most striking differences whereby one individual thing or person is known from another, are differences in *place* (situation, or position), and differences in *time*. The German Ocean probably differs from other oceans in a good many particulars; but most of these are known only to the man of science, the sailor, or the fisherman: to the bulk of persons it is made individual, is distinguished from other oceans, only by its occupying a different place on the map. So to most persons Jerusalem is a separate individual thing only as being the capital of Palestine, and the seat of certain remarkable events. George III. differed from other men in appearance, in movements, in voice, in sayings and doings, and by these differences was known to his acquaintances as a separate individual: but he is best known as King of England from 1760 to 1820, that is by his differences from other Kings in place and in time, which differences are sufficient to make him in their minds a distinct individual.

The skilful teacher will exercise his pupils on this by naming towns, historical personages, &c., and asking whether they are known one from another in any other way than in being on different parts of the map, or in different pages of the history. 'Is Paris Rome?' 'No.' 'How do you know that? Do you know anything more about them than that they are in different positions on the map?' If the pupils read history, they may be exercised in a similar way upon the personages mentioned in what they have been reading. Simple as the exercise appears, the mind may be considerably stirred to thought in illustrating the fundamental fact that we know one thing from another by the differences between them.

Q. 12. When the individual things, as Paris and Rome, are like each other, we are struck with the *agreement*, and think of them together. While Paris and Rome differ in position and in many other respects, they agree in being cities (collections of houses) and in being capital towns. The German Ocean agrees with all other oceans in being a body of salt water, in containing fishes, in being sailed over by ships, &c. When we look around us we see everywhere agreements in the midst of differences: the agreements make things be thought of together, and arranged in our minds into *classes*, while the differences in situation, appearance, &c., make separate *individuals*.

Q. 13. The teacher should frame many questions upon this model: gradually bringing home to the youthful mind the idea that the things around it may be arranged in groups of individuals like each other, yet more or less different.

Q. 14. Here the teacher may repeat and dwell upon the

statement made at the beginning of the section; namely, that all we know about a thing is that it agrees more or less with certain other things, and differs in one point at least from everything else.

The examples in **Exercise** 1 may be given on the black board in a tabulated form—agreements in one list, differences in another. Thus:—

A penny and a shilling

agree

1. in being round and flat
2. in being metals
3. in being coined money.

differ

1. in size
2. in colour.
3. in weight
4. in value

2. A railway and a road *agree* in being used for vehicles to move along, and *differ* in the one having rails for wheels to run on, while the other has not. When this question is put, the pupils may say that the railway is used for steam engines, while an ordinary road is not: in reply to which the teacher will point out that this is not quite correct, as steam engines, called traction engines, are sometimes used on roads. He may also notice that horses are sometimes used to pull waggons on rails: and that sometimes the engine is fixed, and the carriages pulled by a rope.

3. A dwelling-house and a church *agree* in being buildings; *differ* in being used, the one for private purposes, the other for a public purpose, namely, religious worship.

4. Square and triangle—*agree* in being figures enclosed by straight lines; *differ* in form.

5. Food and drink—*agree* in being taken into the stomach for nourishment; *differ* in the consistency of the material—the one being solid, the other liquid.

6. Six and a hundred—*agree* in being numerals; *differ* in the amount they stand for.

7. Arm and leg—*agree* (1) in being limbs, (2) in the number of their joints; *differ* (1) in position, (2) in shape, (3) in function or use.

Eye and ear—*agree* in being organs of sense; *differ* (1) in position, (2) in structure, (3) in use.

8. Dragoon and foot-soldier—*agree* in belonging to the army; *differ* in equipment.

Private and officer—*agree* in belonging to the army; *differ* (1) in rank, (2) in duties.

Lords and Commons—*agree* in being assemblages of men engaged in making laws: *differ* (1) in constitution, the one body being hereditary, the other elective; (2) in various minute powers and privileges.

9. Englishman, Frenchman, German—*agree* in being Europeans: *differ* (1) in abode, (2) in speech, (3) in many small particulars of dress, manners, and way of living.

10. Printing, writing—*agree* in being modes of communicating thought by readable marks: *differ* in the manner of making those marks.

11. Child, man—*agree* in being human creatures: *differ* in the stage of their growth.

12. Catholic, Protestant, Jew, Mahometan—*agree* in being religious sects: *differ* (1) in creed or belief (2) in ritual, or manner of worship.

13. Farmer, builder, merchant—*agree* in being tradesmen or members of trades: *differ* in the nature of their work.

14. Sea, river, fountain—*agree* in being water; and *differ* in the following particulars:—the sea is standing water and salt; a river is running water and fresh; a fountain is water springing from the earth (or from a reservoir).

Desert, field—*agree* in being dry land; *differ* in being (1) the one uncultivated, the other cultivated, (2) the one unproductive, the other productive.

Q. 15. This has been to some extent anticipated. Classes are founded on agreements. Groups of individuals like each other are called classes.

'Stars' agree in being small, twinkling lights, seen in the sky on a clear night; and this agreement is the foundation of the class.

Similarly, 'seas' agree in being vast collections of salt water: 'clouds' in being masses of watery vapour floating in the atmosphere: 'ships' in being large vessels for carrying goods and passengers over seas or up and down rivers; and these several agreements are the foundations of the classes.

Q. 16. A 'General' name is a name that may be applied to any one of a group of similar things; that is, to any individual of a class. Class names and general names have the same meaning. The teacher should take up such class names as 'town,' 'sea,' 'king'; mention individual towns, seas, or kings; and impress upon the pupils that they have a general or common name, because they resemble one another. He may point out the difference between names of this sort, and such names as 'William,' 'George,' 'Charles,' which are applied to persons without regard to their likeness or unlikeness.

Q. 17-21. **Exercise 2.** It is of great importance that pupils should be made familiar with the distinction between Higher and Lower Classes. The teacher should use not only the examples given in the Grammar, but any others that may occur to him as being specially intelligible to the pupils he is dealing with.

In using the Exercise, he may proceed in some such way as follows. On taking up an example, 'social animals,' 'property,' &c., he should first make sure, by close and varied questioning, that the pupils understand the meaning of the terms—What are social animals? Animals that live together, like bees, and not alone or in single pairs, like the lion, the tiger, or the whale. Do social animals form a class? Yes. Why? Because they agree in living together: they resemble each other in this respect, and therefore the general name 'social animal' is given to them. Are 'beavers' a class? Yes—for a similar reason. Is 'social animals' a higher or a lower class than 'beavers'? A higher: because it contains 'beavers' and other classes besides—'bees,' 'wasps,' 'ants.' The class 'social animals' is wider, comprehends a greater number of individuals, than the class 'beavers,' 'bees,' 'wasps,' or 'ants': the general name 'social animal' is applied to a greater number of individuals.

The teacher may also point out that 'animals' is a higher class than 'social animals,' comprehending over and above social animals, all the animals that are not social.

Or going the opposite way in the ladder of classification, he may take the class 'ants,' and mention that it is sub-divided into many classes—yellow ants, red ants, dusky ants, &c.

In explaining degrees of classification, the teacher will find it useful to put upon the black-board such tabulated forms as the following:—

Animals,	*Higher Class.*
Social Animals,	*First Lower.*
Ants,	*Second Lower.*
Yellow Ants,	*Third Lower.*

Taking Ants alone we have—

Ants,	*Higher Class.*
Yellow Ants,	*Lower Class.*

The following more complicated form—the 'tree' form—exhibits to the eye co-ordination as well as subordination:—

Animals.

Social Animals. Solitary Animals.

Beavers, Bees, Ants.

Yellow Ants. Red Ants.

The teacher will farther explain upon these same examples that 'genus' is another name for higher class, 'species' for lower class: that the higher class (or *genus*) contains most individuals, but fewest marks: that a word introducing more marks and so narrowing the class is called an Adjective: that lower classes (or *species*) are called 'subordinate' to their higher classes (or *genera*), while they are called 'co-ordinate' with one another.

Q. 22-24. *Definition.* **Exercise 3.** The simplest way of defining, which the teacher will do well to follow here, is to state the genus or higher class, and then specify the differences.

We are met, however, by a difficulty at starting. In the case of all the classes given for definition in this Exercise, there are several higher classes, at different degrees of comprehensiveness: which shall we mention? The full answer to this would carry us much too far for the present purpose: in these examples the teacher should simply give the class containing all the things enumerated, and thereafter give their differences from each other.

1. Plough, spade, clock, watch, cart, carriage.—All these belong to the *genus* 'machine': they all agree in being mechanical contrivances: they are subordinate to the class machine, and co-ordinate with one another under that class.

So much for what is common to the things: we next consider how they differ from each other. A plough is a machine (1) used for turning up the soil, and (2) dragged by horses. A spade is a machine (1) used for turning up the soil, and (2) worked by hand and foot. A clock is a machine (1) used for marking time, and (2) having a pendulum. A watch is a machine (1) used for marking time, and (2) having a mainspring. A cart is a machine (1) having wheels, and (2) used for conveying goods. A carriage is a machine (1) having wheels, and (2) used for conveying passengers.

These are the differences of the things enumerated viewed as co-ordinate classes under the genus machine. We may take them in smaller groups, under less comprehensive genera, puting a step between, as it were. Thus 'plough' and 'spade' are co-ordinate under the genus agricultural implement, or machine used for turning up the soil: they agree in this. When this is taken as their agreement, when they are looked upon as members of this lower genus, their differences, the points that distinguish the one from the other, are that the one is dragged by horses, while the other is worked by hand and foot. To class them as '*agricultural* machines,' defines or distinguishes them from other machines: to mention these other points defines or distinguishes them from one another.

Similarly 'clock' and 'watch' come under the genus 'timepiece': their chief distinguishing marks being that the one has a pendulum, the other a mainspring. 'Cart' and 'carriage' are co-ordinate under the genus 'wheeled vehicle': the difference being that the one is used for goods, the other for passengers.

The following table represents the two higher grades referred to in the above. They are, as it were, two stories built upon the given classes as a foundation :—

Machines.

Agricultural Implements.	Time-pieces.	Vehicles.
Plough, Spade.	Clock, Watch.	Cart, Carriage.

2. 'Mountain,' 'sea,' and 'lake,' agree in being large physical features. It is part of their definition to say that they are large physical features.

A mountain differs from the other two in being a high elevation of land. It differs from a hill in being higher or larger.

'Sea' and 'lake' differ from a mountain in being sheets or expanses of water: they differ from each other in size.

3. 'Star,' 'planet,' and 'moon,' belong to the class of heavenly bodies.

A star differs from a planet in seeming to us to be fixed: the planet seems to move about, or wander, in a certain course. Both star and planet differ from the moon (1) in apparent size, (2) in movement: the moon is next to the sun in apparent size, and is a satellite of the earth. 'Moon' is not the name of a class, but of an individual body; there is but one moon: 'star' and 'planet' are class names; there are many planets.

4. Builder, sailor, painter, general, king, martyr—agree in being men. We define each of them in the first place by calling him 'a man.'

A builder is a man whose occupation it is to build houses.

A sailor is a man whose occupation it is to attend to the sailing of ships.

A painter is a man whose occupation it is to paint. The term is applied both to trade painters and to Fine Art painters: these are two subordinate classes.

A general is a man that commands an army.

A king is a man that rules a country.

A martyr is a man that has lost his life rather than give up his opinions.

5. 'Book' and 'paper.' A book is a collection of sheets of printed paper *(genus)*, bound together *(difference)*. Co-ordinate classes under the same genus, 'sheets of printed paper,' are newspaper, pamphlet, magazine.

'Paper' is material for writing or printing upon.

6. 'Prudence,' and 'benevolence' belong to the class 'virtues.' Prudence is the virtue of having regard to our own welfare: benevolence, the virtue of having regard to the welfare of others.

Q. 25. 'White' signifies the colour so called as it appears in an object—a horse, a cloth, a piece of paper, a stone: 'whiteness' signifies the colour wherein all white objects agree, spoken of by itself and without regard to any of them in particular. Whiteness is Abstract.

Q. 26—29. WHAT IS SAID OF A SUBJECT—PREDICATION

There is no difficulty in these questions. 'London has a mayor' (Q. 27) is a *Singular* proposition 'all the English towns have mayors' is a *General* proposition. When a proposition is not true in every case, the *Exceptions* should be stated along with it.

Exercise 4. In working this exercise, the teacher would do well to write the Subjects and the Predicates in parallel columns on the black-board, or to ask his pupils to write them out so on slate or paper. Thus :—

Subject.	*Predicate.*
The kettle	boils.
Our neighbour's cat	has taken a rat.
Whoever wishes to be well spoken of	should think what will please other people.
A rose	by any other name would smell as sweet.
The death of Alexander III. of Scotland, by a fall from his horse	was the beginning of great evils to the country.
Great improvements in all kinds of knowledge, and in all the arts	there have been within the last century.

In teaching the youngest pupils to distinguish between Subject and Predicate, one should particularly insist upon, as guiding marks, the questions—What is spoken about? and What is said, or affirmed, about it?

Q. 30-42. The answers to these questions are simply repetitions of what is found in the Grammar. The purpose of the preliminary analysis of Sentences is to bring out clearly the main characters of the several Parts of Speech: and the teacher should insist chiefly upon this.

THE NOUN.

It must be kept in mind that the remarks made in answer to the various questions and in the working out of the exercises, are intended as hints and additional information for the teacher and the private student, and not as specimens of answers to be expected from younger pupils. The teacher must judge for himself at what stage such information should be given to his classes.

In exercising pupils on the Noun, the teacher's first care should be to impress the fundamental notion of the noun as the subject of an affirmation. Every now and again, the pupil should be pulled up, and asked to explain in accordance with the definition, how he knows a word to be a Noun. In answer to this it will be quite enough at first that the pupil recognise the word as *subject* in the sentence given, or frame a sentence having the given Noun as subject. The other distinctions may be reserved to a later stage. The distinction between Noun and Pronoun, should be reverted to when the Pronoun comes up: the final distinction cannot be apprehended till the pupil knows the infinitive forms of the Verb. When all the distinctions have been brought out, such catechising as the following may be found useful :—

Jane waters the flowers. Q. How do you know that 'Jane' is a Noun? A. Because it is the subject of the sentence. Q. How do you know that 'Jane' is not a Pronoun? A. Because it is the name of a person, and not merely a word referring to a name previously mentioned. Q. How do you know that 'Jane' is not the infinitive of a Verb? A. Because it is inflected for case, as in 'Jane's hat,' 'Jane's gloves,' and infinitives are not inflected.

Not to perplex his pupils, whom probably he should not try with this till a tolerably advanced stage, the teacher should tell them that there is no risk of mistaking 'Jane' for an infinitive; and that the purpose of the exercise is simply to make them see that Nouns are sometimes inflected for gender, number, or case, and that is a distinction of the Noun. There is no risk of confusing Noun and Infinitive, except when they have the same form, as occurs with verbal nouns in *ing* 'groaning,' 'sighing,' &c.: in which cases the inflection is a test.

Answers to Questions (p. 41).

It would be superfluous to answer here such of the questions as may be answered by a literal repetition of the words of the grammar. I notice only questions requiring the application of unfamiliar principles. Further, I may say that questions upon the mere text are given only as specimens: they are not intended to be exhaustive, and the skilful teacher will vary them and frame others according as he finds it necessary.

Q. 4. 'Adam,' 'tree,' 'winter,' and such-like are called Nouns, because they may be the subjects or the objects of sentences, affirmations, statements: thus—'*Adam* fell from his first estate;' 'The *tree* is cut up for burning;' '*Winter* is the season of cold.' To show that they correspond fully with the definition, we must show that they differ from Pronouns and from Infinitives, which also may be subjects or objects of sayings, may be spoken about in sentences.

'Adam,' 'tree,' and 'winter,' are names of actual things and so are distinguished from Pronouns. They are distinguished from Infinitives by their inflections: Adam and Winter being inflected for case—'Adam's fall,' 'Winter's snow;' tree for number, 'the trees grow.' At the present stage, the pupil beginning grammar cannot give the full correspondence: he can be expected only to make sentences showing that the given Nouns are used as subjects or as objects. He should be asked to do this on several other Nouns.

Q. 5. The word 'he' is said not to be a Noun, because, though it may stand as the subject of a sentence, it is not the name of an actual thing.

'Great' is not a Noun because it cannot stand as the subject of a sentence. It does not answer the first part of the definition of a Noun.

In such a sentence as 'Loving is more pleasant than hating,' 'loving' is the subject of a sentence. It is also the name of an actual state. It thus answers two parts of the definition of a Noun. But it fails to answer the third: it cannot be inflected either for gender, for number, or for case.

Q. 6. 'India' is unmistakably a Proper noun, as being applied to only one country; but the learner may be puzzled to know why 'Charles' should be called Proper or Singular, seeing that the name is applied to several persons. The truth is that in such cases the titles 'Proper' and 'Singular' are not exactly suitable—at least their suitability is not immediately apparent: and that is the reason why this class of nouns has a third designation, 'Meaningless.' 'Charles,' although a name common to several objects, is yet reckoned in this class, because it is a *Meaningless* mark; used merely to single out an object, and applied to several only from want of singular names, and not on the ground of any likeness or agreement among the objects it is applied to. In the case of such a name as 'Charles,' *Meaningless* is the title to insist upon. Such a name as 'Charles' is common to a number of individuals *without regard to* their being like or unlike each other: a General name is common to a number of individuals *because* they are like each other.

Q. 9. The Nouns 'star,' 'kingdom,' 'table,' are called Common, because *common* to several objects: General, because applicable to every member of a *genus*, or class; Significant, because they *signify* the points wherein the members of a class agree. 'Star' signifies the definition of the class so called, 'a small twinkling light seen in the sky on a clear night.' 'Kingdom' signifies in like manner 'a country ruled by a king.' 'Table' signifies 'an article of household furniture of peculiar construction and peculiar use.'

Q. 10. Class Names are General, as applying to all the members of the class; Significant, for the reason given in answer to Q. 9.

Q. 12. 'Head,' 'family,' and even 'the head of *a* family,' are general designations, class names, applying to several objects in virtue of a common meaning. But 'the head of *our* family' can apply only to one person: the various significant names do not apply unitedly to more than one person.

Similarly, 'father,' and 'mankind,' are significant class names; but in union with the significant words 'the' and 'all,' they apply to one person, and to one alone.

'Stuart,' though not a significant name, is common to a number of individuals: but in union with the other significant words 'the' and 'last,' it applies only to a single individual.

'Pyramid' is a class name: along with 'the' and 'great,' it is restricted to one particular pyramid.

Q. 13. 'Mount' is a class name, signifying 'rising ground.' 'Horeb' is a meaningless name. The two words together make one Singular name.

Similarly, 'falls' is significant; 'Niagara,' meaningless: the two in combination name an individual object.

'St. Paul's' is meaningless, 'cathedral' significant, applying to a certain class of churches. 'St. Paul's Cathedral' is the name of a particular building.

Q. 14. 'People,' 'family,' and 'fleet' are all Significant as well as Collective: 'people' signifies the inhabitants of a country collectively; 'family,' the members of a household collectively; and 'fleet' a number of ships collectively. All these are class names as well as collective names: there are more than one people, more than one family, more than one fleet: and they are thought of together, and named 'peoples, 'families,' and 'fleets,' on account of their common likeness.

Qq. 15, 16. 'Ivory,' 'spice,' and 'grass' are names of Materials: 'wines,' 'spices,' 'grasses,' are class names. This distinction the teacher should exemplify at length; insisting that names of materials are always singular, and that when they are used in the plural, their meaning and their application are changed. Prominence should also be given to the similar fact in the case of Abstract nouns.

Q. 18. 'Education,' 'success,' 'life,' are Abstract: signifying agreements among things, without pointing to any of the things that agree.

Exercise 5.

Singular and General Nouns.

1. 'Columbus'—a strictly Singular and Proper Name. When the word is used by itself, we think only of one individual.

'America'—also strictly Proper, Singular, and Meaningless.

2. 'George Fox'—is not so strictly limited to one person as Columbus. Before we know exactly who is meant, we need the other designation—'the first of the Quakers.'

'Quakers,' though spelt with a capital, is not a Proper Name, but a Class Name, signifying a sect with peculiar doctrines. Every individual professing those doctrines is called by the name.

'The first of the Quakers,' is an example of a Singular Significant name, made up by the union of several General Significant names.

'Shoemaker'—a Class name, signifying 'a man whose trade it is to make shoes.'

3. 'Joan of Arc'—a compound Proper name: Joan being applied to many women, the other designation is added to restrict the name to one.

'Stake,' a general significant name, here used in a peculiar way. Generally it signifies any long thin piece of wood sharpened at one end and driven into the ground: here, by what is called a Figure of Speech, it signifies, as it were, the particular stake that martyrs were bound to when they were burnt to death.

4. 'Washington,' a Meaningless word, here used as the name of a town. It is used also as the name of a man. When we see the name by itself, we do not know which is intended; either another designation must be added, such as 'the Ame-

rican patriot,' or 'the capital &c.,' or we must guess from what is said about it.

'United States,' is an example of a Singular Name, having at present a certain meaning or significance. 'The capital of the United States,' is a general name, 'capital,' restricted to one place by an additional designation. There are many capitals; there is only one capital of the United States.

5. 'Ark' and 'covenant' are both General names: but the combination 'the ark of the covenant,' is Singular, applies only to one thing.

'Mount Zion' is a Mixed Singular name; 'mount' is significant, 'Zion' meaningless.

6. 'Roman Catholics' are, like 'Quakers,' a class: the name is general, and significant of peculiar doctrines.

'The Blessed Virgin' is a Significant Singular designation.

'Flesh,' is a noun of Material.

'Lent,' is a Proper noun, the name of a festival.

7. 'Shout,' General, Significant.

'Reign,' Abstract, Significant.

'Chaos,' and 'Night,' are, like 'Providence,' Singular and Significant. They are Abstract nouns, treated as persons.

8. 'Earth,' also Singular and Significant. It is a noun of Material, treated as a person.

9. 'Laud,' Proper name. There may be many persons of that name, but when it stands by itself, we know the individual meant.

'Tower,' is a general name, restricted by the article 'the' to one particular place.

10. 'Christmas,' Proper name, a festival. Originally it

was significant, 'Christ's mass,' but now it has the force only of a meaningless mark.

11. 'Measles,' 'Scarletina,' 'Small-pox'—Proper names, diseases. It is hard to decide in what class names of diseases should be reckoned. They are certainly not used as Class Names: we do not speak of a Measles, a Small-pox, or a Scarletina. Nor are they Collective.

12. 'James,' 'Mary,' are Meaningless, but applied to many different persons, and needing some other designation before they denote only one person without risk of confusion.

'Arithmetic,' and 'Music,' are Singular or Proper names, denoting branches of knowledge.

'January' is a Proper name, denoting a month.

Exercise 6.

Nouns generally.

1. 'Frederick the Great,' a Meaningless Proper name restricted to one particular person by a significant epithet.

'Empire,' is used sometimes as an Abstract noun, sometimes as a General noun. 'The Empire' is a Singular and Significant name.

'The Seven Years' War,' is a Singular and Significant name, comprising two General nouns, 'year,' and 'war.'

2. 'Kindness,' an Abstract noun, formed from the adjective 'kind.'

'Animals,' a General noun. 'Kindness to animals' is the subject of the sentence. 'Animals' is an example of a noun occurring along with a preposition, in a phrase.

'Exercise,' an Abstract noun, formed from a verb :'benevolence,' an Abstract noun, formed from an adjective.

3. 'Produce,' an Abstract noun, formed from a verb. 'Labour,' an Abstract noun. 'Produce' may be called a passive verbal abstract, standing as it does for 'what is produced:' 'labour' an active verbal abstract, standing in place of the active infinitive 'labouring.'

'Wealth,' an Abstract noun, formed from an adjective. 'Produce,' 'labour,' and 'wealth' are examples of three well-marked classes of Abstract nouns, the passive verbal abstract, the active verbal abstract, and the adjectival abstract. This is probably too fine a distinction for younger pupils, but the teacher should try how far it can be explained to them. The distinguishing of the different classes of Noun is the best discipline of the ingenuity that Grammar affords, the exercise that most calls for thought, and is least liable to be made a matter of barren mechanical routine.

4. 'Security,' an adjectival Abstract noun.

'Property,' an adjectival Abstract noun, sometimes used in the plural, in which case it is a General noun.

'Capital,' is an Abstract noun, meaning 'money' or 'goods' viewed as a starting-point for producing more. Both 'property' and 'capital' have something of the 'Material' as well as of the 'Collective' in them: each stands for a collection of materials viewed in a certain relation. This distinction should probably be reserved for more advanced classes.

'Power,' and 'skill,' are Abstract nouns, having adjectives corresponding to them.

'Combination,' 'division,' and 'self-preservation,' are active verbal Abstracts.

5. 'Throne,' a General noun, here restricted by significant epithets to one particular throne. The teacher may perhaps remark that the word is used in what is called a Figure of

Speech: the throne is represented as doing what only a living being could do.

'Cæsars,' a Proper, Meaningless noun: applying to several persons holding the same office, and so used in the Plural. This is an example of a Proper name originally meaningless, but in course of time coming to have an approach to a meaning, being really significant of a certain dignity or rank.

'Certainty,' an adjectival Abstract noun; 'possession,' an active verbal Abstract noun.

'Occupier,' a General noun.

6. 'Dirt' and 'matter' are nouns of Material; 'place,' a General noun.

7. 'Agents,' a General noun. The teacher may here, if he thinks fit, explain the force of the Possessive Case. The pupil would probably carry away only that *'s* is the sign of the Possessive Case; still, that would be so much anticipated. Such anticipations, which the teacher should make at his discretion, gradually take away the burden of absolute novelty, and make the pupil's task lighter as he proceeds.

'Speed,' an Abstract noun, having a corresponding adjective 'speedy.'

'Turf,' a noun of Material.

'Height,' 'thickness,' adjectival Abstract nouns.

'Space,' an Abstract noun (see Gram. p. 37).

'Half,' an Abstract noun.

'Acre,' a General noun.

'Rampart,' a General noun.

'Arms,' 'ammunition,' and 'provisions,' are nouns of Material. So far they are, like 'property,' and 'capital,' Collective; being names for heterogeneous collections of things used for a common purpose. The names signifying only the purpose of the various articles embraced under each, they may also be said to be Abstract. 'Arms,' and 'provisions,' are used only in the *Plural* (which designation the teacher has probably already seen reason to explain).

'Settlement,' originally an Abstract noun, active verbal: here used as a General noun.

'Plank,' a noun of Material.

8. 'Time' (see Gram. p. 37).

'Foot,' 'horse,' Collective nouns.

9. 'Lowliness,' adjectival Abstract noun.

'Ambition,' originally an Abstract noun; here used as a Singular noun, by a figure of speech called Personification.

10. 'Grape,' 'gooseberry,' General nouns. Here, by a peculiar effect of 'the,' they are converted into Collective nouns: 'the grape,' 'the gooseberry,' are names for 'grapes' and 'gooseberries' collectively.

'Fruit,' like 'ammunition,' a sort of Collective noun of Material. Here it is used as a General noun (see Gram. p. 36).

11. 'Affectation,' verbal Abstract noun.

'Part,' an abstract noun, here used as a general noun.

'Behaviour,' an active verbal Abstract.

'Defects.' 'Defect' is an Abstract noun, but here, as the plural indicates, it is used as a General noun.

The teacher may remark concerning 'lighting up' that it is an example of an infinitive occurring in one of the places where a noun might occur (Gram. p. 38). In the following sentence it is the subject:—'Lighting up a candle to our defects is injudicious.'

12. 'Beauties,' Abstract, used as General; 'poem,' General; 'sight,' Abstract, active verbal, equivalent to 'act of seeing.'

13. 'Life' is an Abstract noun, as also 'liberty:' but in the second clause, they are used as General nouns, in the plural. Some authorities object to this usage, holding that we should say 'their life,' and 'their liberty.'

14. 'Geometry,' Singular noun, name of a branch of knowledge: 'practice,' Abstract, active verbal: 'perfection,' Abstract, adjectival: 'sciences,' and 'arts,' General. 'Science' and 'Art' are originally Abstract: they are also often used as Singular names for large departments of knowledge.

15. 'Set,' a Collective noun: 'ferns,' General: 'district,' General, originally Abstract.

16. 'A property.' According to the rule (see Gram. p. 37) 'property' is here a General noun.

'Societies,' a Collective noun used in the plural.

For the other words, see No. 4.

17. 'Loam,' 'sand,' 'clay,' are nouns of Material. In 'potter's' (a General noun) we have another example of the Possessive.

18. 'Hundreds,' a Collective noun, used in the plural: 'grasses,' a noun of Material, used in the plural, and so converted into a General or Class noun: 'Botany,' a Proper, or Singular noun, name of a branch of knowledge.

'Work' is here General. It is originally, like 'labour,' an abstract noun.

19. 'Halloween,' 'Shrove Tuesday,' Singular nouns, names of Festivals; like 'Christmas,' originally significant.

20. 'Morris,' a Singular name.

'Saddle,' a General noun.

'People,' a Collective noun.

'Old Treasurer,' a compound Singular name; a good example of significant names applied without any meaning to designate an individual.

'Fraction,' an Abstract noun.

'Regiment,' 'battery,' 'squadron,' Collective nouns.

21. 'Humanity,' Abstract, adjectival.

'Creatures,' a General noun: originally a passive verbal abstract.

'Reason,' an Abstract noun.

22. 'Cholera,' Singular noun, name of disease: 'ravages,' here a General noun, originally Abstract, active, verbal.

23. 'Lime,' noun of Material.

'Ingredient,' General noun.

'Soils,' here a General noun, meaning kinds or varieties of soil; originally a noun of Material (see Gram. p. 36).

24. 'Front,' an Abstract noun.

'Ranks,' here a Collective noun, denoting the men ranked in a body. 'Rank,' in the singular, is an Abstract noun, a passive verbal, like 'produce,' meaning 'what is ranked,' without regard to anything but the fact that it is ranked.

'Charge,' an Abstract noun.

'Russian,' a General noun, not a proper name, though spelt with a capital. 'Russian' means 'an inhabitant of Russia,' and is a general name for every such inhabitant.

'Squadron-leader,' a General noun.

25. 'The Arminian controversy,' 'the English Government,' 'the English Church,' 'the Calvinistic party,' are examples of Singular names formed by the combination of several significant names.

'Controversy,' and 'support,' are Abstract nouns: 'government,' 'church,' and 'party,' are Collective nouns. 'Holland' is a strictly Singular noun, a name for a single country: we cannot apply it to any other place without an epithet, as '*New* Holland.' The same word is also a family name, and a name of material (fine linen); and 'hollands' is a name for Dutch gin: but when 'Holland' is used alone, we at once think of the country so called.

26. 'March,' 'April,' Singular nouns, names of months: 'the Houses of Parliament,' a mixed Singular name, like 'Exeter Hall,' partly significant, partly meaningless. 'Parliament' itself was originally significant, but it has lost its meaning, and is now a meaningless designation for the supreme council of the English nation. It is sometimes used as a General noun by a figure of speech.

27. 'Carbon,' noun of Material: 'element,' General: 'plants,' General.

28. 'Wheat,' noun of Material: 'grain,'—see No. 10, 'fruit:' 'oats,' a simple noun of Material, though plural in form.

29. 'Frost,' Abstract noun: 'appearance,' Abstract, active verbal: 'the northern lights,' a Singular name, made by a combination of significant names, one of them (an unusual case) plural: 'certainty,' abstract.

30. 'Report,' an Abstract noun, here used as a General noun.

'Committee,' Collective noun, restricted by the adjective 'Select,' and the phrase 'of the House of Commons.'

'The House of Commons,' see above, No. 26, 'the Houses of Parliament.'

'State,' 'education,' 'amount,' 'information,' 'increase,' 'decency,' 'deportment,' are all Abstract nouns.

THE PRONOUN.

Answers to Questions—(p. 55).

Q. 1. The Pronoun—

Agrees with the Noun in the following :—

I. *Essential Points.*

1. It may be Subject or Object of a sentence.
2. It may be inflected for Gender, Number, or Case.

II. *Minor Points.*

1. It may be used with a Preposition to make a phrase.
2. It may be used to complete a Predicate.
3. It is sometimes used instead of an Adjective: as in '*he*-goat,' '*she*-goat.'

Differs from the Noun in the following :—

1. It does not name an Object, but refers to a name.

The above is a full scheme of the agreements and differences between the Pronoun and the Noun. The first agreement alone may be considered enough for the beginner. It may be said in general terms that the Pronoun has all the defining marks of the Noun except that it refers and does not name.

Q. 2. Generally speaking, to see whom 'he' denotes, we must look to what has gone before. Occasionally, the word referred to comes after, as—'*He* fell in her arms, *the poor wounded hussar.*'

Q. 3. In applying the definition to the Personal Pronouns, the great point to impress is that they are not names of actual objects, and that before we know whom or what they designate, we must look to the circumstances. The small print in Grammar, p. 42, is a specimen of the sort of explanation required. Of course, in applying the definition to this or to any other class of Pronouns, the teacher may, if he thinks it necessary, repeat all the points of agreement and difference tabulated in answer to Q. 1.

Q 4. This question is a sample of questions very useful in bringing out what may be called the referential character of the Pronouns.—Who are denoted by *we?* The person speaking and his associates. '*You* are too anxious'—Who are denoted by *you?* The persons addressed. If we open a page of a book, and find the pronoun 'I,' do we know at once who is denoted? No. Where do we look to discover who it is; what do we refer to? We refer to the title-page to see the name of the writer of the book."

Q. 7. The first-named reference of 'it' is uncertain, when two nouns go before, either of which may be the one referred to. In such cases we have no means of deciding the true reference, except by considering the sense of the passage.

To help the memory, the teacher may write the various modes of reference of 'it' upon the black-board, in some such form as this:—

MODES OF REFERENCE OF THE PRONOUN 'IT.'

I. *Backward* Reference,
   (1) to a single word,
   (2) to a clause.

II. *Forward* Reference,
   to a phrase or a clause.

III. *Indefinite* Reference.

Q. 13. 'One' and 'they' are the chief Indefinite Demonstratives. 'Other' is also pretty frequently used. In the larger Grammar (p. 21), several adjectives are enumerated that are used in almost the same way.

Q. 14. In such expressions as—'One does not know what to do in such a position,' 'one' is thoroughly Indefinite in its reference, pointing to nothing in the context, either before or after: any special reference that it has is to the person speaking or the person addressed, in which cases it is an inoffensive substitute for a Personal pronoun. In this use it may be called an Indefinite Personal pronoun. In the other use it is more of a Numeral pronoun, with a reference back:—'How very nice those story-books are; I should like to have *one*.' In this last case, however, the reference is also indefinite: it is not one particular book that is wanted, but any one. The difference between the two uses may be succinctly stated thus:—In the first case, 'one' is a politely Indefinite Personal pronoun, with no reference to the context; in the second case, 'one' is an indefinite Numeral pronoun, with a reference back to the context.

Q. 15. 'The one is deaf, the *other* blind.' In the saying—He has *other* property, 'other' is not a Pronoun, but an Adjective. The Pronoun stands alone, the Adjective takes a noun along with it.

Q. 17. A Relative pronoun, besides referring to an object like a Personal or a Demonstrative pronoun, serves the purpose of uniting sentences, or clauses, like a Conjunction. 'John, *who* is usually a steady shot, missed the target four times running.' Here 'who,' referring back to John, and so answering the definition of a Pronoun, unites two sentences, and so is distinguished from other Pronouns. This function of uniting two sentences is the Relative's peculiar 'difference' or distinction among the Pronouns.

Qq. 19-21. The teacher should take pains to enforce the distinction between co-ordination and restriction. To say that two co-ordinated statements are independent of each other, have no connection at all, would be putting it too strongly. Perhaps the remark most intelligible and best fitted to bring out the distinction, is that the Restrictive statement, the sentence or clause introduced by the Restrictive relative, is necessary to signify who or what is denoted by the word referred to, the antecedent; while on the other hand, the Co-ordinate statement, the sentence or clause introduced by the Co-ordinating relative, is some additional information about a person or thing already known. The expression 'the man,' does not signify definitely a certain individual: we need the Restrictive clause 'that I called on,' merely to complete the designation: 'the man that I called on,' is all required to name the individual. So with other examples of Restrictive clauses. On the other hand, the expression, 'The Duke of Wellington,' is sufficient to denote the individual: the clause, 'who commanded the English armies in the Peninsula,' gives additional information. This information may be said to be co-ordinate with the information of the other member of the sentence, 'never lost a battle;' that is to say, neither statement is required to let us know who is signified by 'The Duke of Wellington.'

Q. 22. 'We pursue *what* pleases us,'—*the thing that* pleases us, or *the things that* please us. Though 'what' is singular, it may have a plural reference.

Q. 23. 'Such as,' and 'but' are always restrictive: 'when,'

'where,' and 'whence,' are sometimes restrictive, sometimes co-ordinating.

'It is a nice situation for *such as* love variety'—such persons as the persons *that* love variety.

'There is no man but likes to have respect shown to him;' *that* does *not* like. 'But' is equivalent to '*that* not,' and always comes after a negative. The full expression of the meaning is—'There is no man but *the man that* likes to have respect shown to him:' that is, excluding all such men, you have no man left.

Q. 24. An Interrogative pronoun is virtually a Relative pronoun with the antecedent or word referred to left indefinite. It is a real Pronoun, inasmuch as it indicates by a reference: it refers to some person, thing, or fact unknown, and which the questioner wishes to be known.

Exercise 7.

Pronouns generally.

The teacher will do well to make his pupils distinguish all the Nouns as well as the Pronouns in these Exercises. Generally, in each Exercise, the pupils should be drilled to the full extent of their previous knowledge.

1. 'The evils that it has caused,' 'the evils that it has removed.' The two *its* are examples of the first reference of 'it,' the backward reference to a single word, that word (the 'antecedent') being 'revolution.' The *thats* are here properly Restrictive in both cases: the whole phrase is required to signify the evils intended; the whole class of evils is narrowed or restricted to these smaller classes, 'the evils caused by a revolution,' and 'the evils removed by a revolution.'

2. 'That' is here also the correct relative: the clause 'that was full of people' is designed to point us to one particular city. If the expression had been—'Jerusalem, which was full of people, is now solitary;' the clause would have been co-ordinate, and 'which' the proper Relative: Jerusalem fully designating the city of that name, and the clause giving us additional information. In that case, to use the other Relative—'*that* was full of people,' would have implied that there were more than one Jerusalem, and that this fact was necessary to distinguish the one from the other.

3. 'They say,' an example of 'they' as an Indefinite Demonstrative.

'This' is here a Pronoun: we may, if we please, parse it as an Adjective with 'place understood, but the usage is essentially pronominal—it expresses a place by a reference to the position of the speaker or writer.

'It' refers back to the whole preceding clause.

4. 'Which' here refers to the action of crossing the Pruth.

5. 'What,' equivalent to 'the thing that.'

6. The only difficulty among these simple Pronouns is the reference of 'it'—'as he was fortunate, I rejoice at *it*.' The antecedent of 'it' is 'the fact that he was fortunate' (Mode of Reference I. 2).

7. We have no means of knowing the reference of 'him.' 'That' refers to the whole preceding question.

8. 'What' is here not a Pronoun, but an Adjective, having the noun 'sign' along with it. The reference of 'it' is somewhat indefinite; being a forward reference to the whole subsequent clause.

9. 'Such as,' a restrictive relative, the full expression being 'such a prize as *the prize that*.'

'It,' backward reference to single word.

'That,' restrictive relative, antecedent 'prize.'

'I.' To make younger pupils familiar with the idea, the teacher should ask—What is the reference of 'I'? or, Whom does 'I' refer to? the answer expected being—the person speaking. So with the other Personal Pronouns, as 'them' and 'us' in the next example. If there is no antecedent given, we have no means of knowing who it is that third personal pronouns refer to; but the first and the second, representing the person or persons addressing and the person or persons addressed, can always be assigned.

10. 'It,' forward reference to clause—'that much was useful &c.'

'That,' restrictive. '*Which* was useful,' would here be wrong.

11. 'That,' a demonstrative pronoun. This is one of the few constructions where 'that' is undeniably pronominal: we cannot well in this case suppose a noun understood, and treat 'that' as an adjective.

'Themselves,' reflective demonstrative.

12. This sentence from Scott contains a correct use of the co-ordinating relative. 'The willow' is sufficient to let us know the object intended: 'which bends to the tempest,' is a statement about an object already in our eye. So with 'the oak,' and its co-ordinating relative. To say—'the willow *that* bends to the tempest,' would imply that there are varieties of willow, and that this circumstance of bending to the tempest distinguishes one of them.

There are two possible antecedents to 'it;' namely, 'willow' and 'tempest.' We know, from the sense, that 'tempest' is the real one.

13. A sentence from Matthew Arnold, illustrating the repetition of the indefinite personal demonstrative 'one.'

14. Reference of 'he' is unknown, so far as the text shows. The sentence is from Addison, and the affirmation is made concerning 'the man of taste,' to whom, therefore, 'he' refers.

'As *it* were,' 'it' of indefinite reference.

'Discovers in *it*,' reference I. 1, antecedent 'world.'

15. 'This,' having a noun along with it, is here an adjective.

16. 'It,' forward reference to the clause—'that one begins to consider, &c.'

'When' is here a relative adverb, not a pronoun.

18. '*But* was,' equivalent to '*that* was *not*.' There is always a negative before 'but' when it is used for a relative: perhaps, indeed, we should state the usage by saying that 'nothing but was,' is equivalent to 'nothing that was not.'

19. 'Himself,' 'others,' and 'they,' will all be easily recognised. We know from the sense that the antecedent of 'they' is 'thoughts:' there is nothing in the form to prevent its being 'others.'

20. 'It,' forward reference to clause—'that you, my boy &c.'

'You, my boy,' an instance of the word referred to being actually supplied. 'You,' is here, of course, singular.

'Where,' equivalent to '*that* . . . *in*:' the equivalent of a restrictive relative.

'Myself.' In parsing these Reflectives, the pupil should be made to say whether they are Demonstrative or First or Second Personal.

21. This illustrates the distinction between the co-ordinating and the restrictive relatives. The clauses accompanying 'morass' are supposed merely to fill out an idea already partially given by the word; the clause attached to landscape singles out a particular kind of landscape.

22. 'It,' forward reference to the clause that states the confession—'that great and splendid actions &c.'

'That leaves no room for them,' is a restrictive clause, narrowing the general extent of the word 'system,' to systems of a special kind.

'They,' simple backward reference.

'Where,' has here a similar force to what it has in No. 20.

23. 'Which are themselves.' Had 'that' been used, the effect would have been to restrict the class animals to such as are incapable of art, implying that certain animals are capable of art, and that in their case nature is superseded.

24. 'No writer *but* must,' 'no writer *that* must *not*.' 'But' an equivalent for the restrictive relative and a negative.

25. A good example of 'that' as an unquestionable pronoun referring back to all that precedes. In '*this* downfall,' 'this' is an adjective.

26. 'But' is not properly a relative here, but a conjunction equivalent to the conjunction 'that' followed by 'not'—'no cliff is so bare *that* on its steep thy favours may *not* be found.' It would be an error to take 'cliff' as the antecedent of 'but,' though one is inclined to do so at first sight.

27. The 'that not' equivalent of 'but' is here properly relative.

28. Illustrates the forward reference of 'it' to a clause, and the latitude allowed to 'it' as a word of reference. It here refers to a person, in an indefinite way.

29. The clause introduced by 'that' particularises 'the raven;' restricts the class to one particular individual.

30. 'Who' introduces a strictly co-ordinate clause, a clause that does nothing to render the application of the antecedent 'host' more particular, but makes a statement about an individual already particularised.

31. A similar remark may be made about 'which' in this sentence.

THE ADJECTIVE.

Answers to Questions—(p. 73).

Q. 1. In applying the definition of the Adjective to any particular Adjective, our plan must be to choose a Noun and show how this is increased in meaning and limited in extent by the given Adjective.

Take, for example, the noun 'eye' and the adjective 'bright.' When 'bright' is joined to 'eye,' the expression—'bright eye'—means more than 'eye' alone, and applies to fewer objects: to have a bright eye is more than to have simply an eye, and fewer persons have bright eyes. The word 'bright,' having thus the effect of increasing the meaning and narrowing the application, is called an adjective.

Similarly, 'a square pane' means more than 'a pane' simply, but there are fewer 'square panes' than 'panes.' So the expression—'a good man,' lets us know more than the expression, 'a man,' but it applies to fewer individuals. In all such cases the extra word adds to the meaning of the noun, but at the same time it makes the noun applicable to fewer individuals. It is called an Adjective as being a word 'thrown to' a noun.

Q. 2. The Adjective is distinguished from the Noun in not being admissible as Subject or Object of a Sentence. The Sentence is separated into two great divisions—Subject and Predicate: the leading word in the first of these divisions is the Noun. The adjective is but a helping word, a subordinate; it cannot by itself be a subject; it merely adds to the meaning of the Noun.

This is the broad distinction. When the pupil comes to Inflection, he will find minuter differences. Nouns are inflected for Gender, Number, and Case: Adjectives are inflected only for Degree.

The same points distinguish the Adjective from the Pronoun.

Q. 3. The teacher should write a scheme of the Classes on the black-board, thus:—

I. Pronominal Adjectives.
  1. Demonstratives.
  2. Possessives.

II. Adjectives of Quantity.
  1. Quantity in Mass or Bulk.
  2. Quantity in Number.
    (1) Definite Numerals.
    (2) Indefinite Numerals.
    (3) Distributive Numerals.

III. Adjectives of Quality.
  Time, Space, Form, Motion, Solidity, Fluidity, Colour, Good and Evil, &c.
  Proper Adjectives.

By way of exercise, he might single out a class, and ask the pupil to mention individual words contained under it: or mention a word, and ask under what class it comes.

Adjectives of Quality are by far the most numerous class.

Q. 4. In showing that Pronominal Adjectives come under the definition, we follow the same plan as before. Take the noun 'book.' We add to the meaning of the word when we call it 'my book,' or 'his book,' or 'this book;' and we consequently narrow the application. Only a limited number of books can be called 'my book' or 'his book,' and 'this book' can be applied but to one at a time.

Q. 5. 'This' and 'that' are called *correlative* words because when one of them is applied to a word, we know that the other cannot be applied at the same time. The same book cannot be at once 'this book,' and 'that book.' 'Up' and 'down,' 'long' and 'short,' 'straight' and 'crooked,' are similar *correlative* pairs. A thing may be 'crooked,' and 'hard,' and 'yellow,' and 'sweet;' these words are not *correlative:* but it cannot be both 'crooked' and 'straight.'

Q. 6. Your, his, its, their—are called Pronominal Possessive Adjectives, because they are the possessives of pronouns.

Q. 7. 'Much' and 'great,' are Adjectives of Quantity in Mass or Bulk. 'Some' and 'any' are Adjectives of Quantity in Mass in such expressions as 'some food,' 'any water;' Adjectives of Quantity in Number (Indefinite) in such expressions as 'some houses,' 'any trees.'

We show that they comply with the definition as before, upon such instances as 'much pleasure,' 'great sorrow,' 'some houses,' 'any trees:' in all which cases the Noun by itself means less and applies to a greater number of individual cases.

To show that they cannot be Nouns we may point out that they are not used as subjects or as objects of sentences. This we can do for 'much,' 'great,' and 'any.' But in such a sentence as—'*Some* consented, others would not,' 'some' appears as the subject of a verb. Applying, therefore, the second test in the definition of the Noun, we see that 'some' is not a Noun, not being the name of an actual thing. Is it then a Pronoun? Does it name a thing or things by a reference? In such cases probably it may be put down, like 'others,' as an Indefinite Demonstrative Pronoun. If not, it must be considered as an Adjective with its Noun 'persons' understood.

Q. 8. 'Five,' 'third,' 'triple,' are Adjectives of Quantity, Definite Numeral; five—*cardinal*, third—*ordinal*, triple—*multiplying*. They may be shown to comply with the definition in such instances as 'five apples,' 'the third row,' 'triple allowance;' which expressions mean more, and are applied less widely than 'apples,' 'row,' 'allowance.'

Q. 11. 'Either' is often misapplied for 'each.' It is incorrect to say—'There is a pillar on *either* side of the gate,' when we mean that there are two pillars, one on each side: the proper word is 'each.' 'Either' means one of two, *but not both.* Milton's expression—

Before Hell's gate there sat
On either side a formidable shape—

is incorrect: 'each side' is the correct grammar, though it would make wrong metre.

Q. 13. To apply the definition, all that is necessary is to quote instances where the given Adjectives occur along with Nouns, and to point out that they have the effect stated as the defining mark of the Adjective. The teacher should make sure that the pupils understand as clearly as possible what is meant by narrowing the class and increasing the meaning: the idea so simple to a grown up person may be a little perplexing to the youthful mind. The narrowing of the class is perhaps the simplest idea: and the easiest way of approaching this is to point out that you apply the noun (*e.g.* man) to everything called by that name, while you can apply the noun along with the adjective (*e.g.* tall man) to only a section, a portion, of the things called by the name.

Q. 14. 'Old' is not a Pronominal Adjective, nor is it an Adjective of Quantity: it is therefore an Adjective of Quality. Similarly with 'rapid,' 'smooth,' and 'pleasant.'

Q. 15. Proper Adjectives are classed among Adjectives of Quality in the same way: they are neither Pronominal Adjectives, nor Adjectives of Quantity, therefore they are considered Adjectives of Quality.

Q. 16, 17. The examples here may be treated like those in the Grammar. '*The* man,' is some particular man that we have been talking of or otherwise denoting; '*the* table,' some particular table that we have for the time to do with; '*the* church,' the church that we are in the habit of attending.

Q. 18. The teacher should write these on the black-board in column, thus:—

1. An Adjective Clause.
2. A Participial Phrase.
3. A Noun.
4. A Prepositional Phrase.
5. A Possessive Case.
6. An Adverb.

Q. 19. 'The man *that is* rich.'

Q. 20. The Participial Phrase either is or resembles a shortened Adjective Clause. It is derived from the Clause by omitting the relative and changing the verb into a Participle, thus—Every man *that has* an interest (Clause); Every man *having* an interest (Part. Phrase).

Q. 21. 'London Weekly Express.' 'London' and 'Weekly, as they stand, are used as Adjectives. Ordinarily, 'London' is a noun, and 'weekly' an adverb. The expression may be viewed as a compression, condensation, or shortening of clauses: the full expression being—*The* Express *that is published* weekly *in* London.

Q. 22. A Prepositional Phrase standing in place of an adjective, as—'the cottage *by the sea,*' is properly viewed as an Adverbial phrase (or phrase used instead of an Adverb), qualifying a verb understood, as—'the cottage *situated* (or *built*) by the sea.' The Participial Phrase being viewed as a contraction of the Adjective Clause, the Prepositional Phrase is a still farther contraction, the verb, as well as the relative, being omitted altogether from the full expression—the cottage that is situated by the sea.

Q. 23. On a similar principle the Possessive Case also is viewed as a contraction from the Clause: Jacob's ladder=the ladder *that was seen by* Jacob; Time's revenge=the revenge *that is taken by* Time.

Q. 24. As in the case of the Prepositional Phrase—the equivalent of an Adverb, so in the case of the Adverb itself, when used in place of an Adjective, we suppose an omission of a Verb: thus—the *early* bird=the bird *that is awake* early.

Q. 25. The fields are wet; the road is dirty; the fence is strong. The Verb in such cases is incomplete, conveys no meaning without the Adjective.

Q. 26. A Restrictive Adjective is an adjective that narrows the application of a noun, *restricts* it to a smaller class or to an individual: whereas a Co-ordinate Adjective adds to the meaning without narrowing or otherwise affecting the extent of the class. An Adjective in the Predicate must always be co-ordinate, because the class is always specified in the words of the Subject, indeed, *is* the Subject: the purpose of the Predicate is not to restrict, but to make a statement about a class already restricted. 'Marine animals are cold'—the adjective 'cold' does not restrict the subject 'marine animals, but adds a fact about them: the expression 'cold marine animals' applies to just the same number of individuals as 'marine animals.' Similarly in the other example; 'costly' does not restrict, but adds or co-ordinates; 'costly old wine' is applicable to everything that 'old wine' is applicable to.

The Predicate Adjective can restrict only a noun expressed or understood in the Predicate. In the above examples, 'cold' restricts 'animals' understood in the Predicate: 'costly' restricts 'wine' understood. The class 'cold animals' is smaller than the class 'animals;' 'costly wine' is of narrower application than 'wine:' but the class 'cold animals' is not narrower than the class 'marine animals;' nor is 'costly wine' of narrower application than 'old wine.'

Q. 27. An Adjective going along with a Proper or Singular name cannot be restrictive. The Singular name already denotes an individual, and its application cannot be farther restricted. The adjective in such a case must superadd meaning, that is, must be Co-ordinate.

Exercise 8—(p. 60).

Pronominal Adjectives.

This Exercise is prescribed for Pronominal Adjectives, but others occur, and these are here referred to their classes. The teacher may go back upon the Exercise when he has taken his pupils over the remaining classes.

1. 'This,' Pronominal demonstrative: 'its,' Pronominal possessive.

'One,' Adj. of Quantity, definite numeral: 'all,' Adj. of Quantity, indefinite numeral: 'firm,' Adj. of Quality, solidity.

2. 'That,' Pronominal demonstrative: 'our,' Pronominal possessive.

'*Spear* wound.' This is an example of a noun used as an adjective. It may be viewed as a contraction for 'wound *made by a* spear.'

3. 'Those,' 'that,' Pronominal demonstratives, plural and singular.

'Rugged,' Adj. of Quality, form: 'yew-tree's,' a Possessive Case, a substitute for an Adjective—yew-tree's shade=shade made by a yew-tree.

4. An example to show the use of 'this' and 'that' as correlatives or contrasting words. The teacher might ask—What are 'this' and 'that' said to be when used in this way?

'Open,' Adj. of Quality, properly used concerning space, here used in what is called a figure of speech.

5. 'Yon,' Pronominal demonstrative: 'her,' Pronominal possessive.

'Own' may be parsed separately as an Adjective of Quality, but really it is never used but with the Possessive Pronouns, to make up an intensified form.

6. 'Yonder,' Pronominal demonstrative.

7. 'Their,' 'your,' Pronominal possessives. 'Yours,' is the predicate form of 'your:' here, however, it is not in the predicate. This is an example of another use of 'yours' instead of 'your;' namely, when the noun it restricts has

occurred before, and is not repeated with it. In such a position it is really as much a pronoun as an Adjective. The following are other examples of the same usage of Possessive Adjectives :—My coat is brown, yours is black : his horses are grey, theirs are chesnut : his eyes were dark, hers were light blue.

8. 'This,' Pronominal demonstrative : 'his,' Pronominal possessive.

Exercise 9—(p. 62).

Adjectives of Quantity.

1. 'Small,' 'great,' Mass or Bulk.

2. 'Enormous,' Mass or Bulk.

3. 'Every,' Distributive Numeral : 'little,' Mass or Bulk.

4. 'Much,' Mass or Bulk : 'forty,' and 'three,' Definite Numerals, *Cardinal.* 'Another,' is so far a Definite Numeral, meaning '*one* other' : but it is also so far indefinite, inasmuch as it means '*any* one other.'

5. 'Seven,' Definite Numeral, *Cardinal :* 'fifteenth,' 'seventh,' Definite Numerals, *Ordinal.*

6. 'All,' 'few,' Indefinite Numerals.

7. 'Several,' here a Distributive Numeral. Upon such an opportunity as this, the pupil should be asked to give an example of 'several' used as an Indefinite Numeral, such as —'It is *several* days since I have seen you :' 'several trees are in blossom.'

'Each.' The pupil should here be passed through some such drill as is given in answer to Q. 11.

8. 'The two large rods.' Here we have an example of three Adjectives used together for the purpose of restricting

or specifying. 'Large' restricts as regards the Mass or Bulk: 'two' restricts as regards the Number: and the definite article 'the,' a weakened form of the demonstrative 'that,' calls attention to certain 'two large rods' in particular.

'*Either* of the two,' implies that I do not want both: had 'each' been used, the meaning would have been that both were wanted.

9. 'The five rooms on the second floor.' 'Five,' a Definite numeral, is here an example of a co-ordinate Adjective. 'The rooms on the second floor,' is sufficient for purposes of restriction: this expression alone lets us know the rooms intended. That they are five in number is a piece of extra information, *co-ordinated* by the Adjective 'five.' 'On the second floor,' is a prepositional phrase, used in place of an Adjective; the full expression being—'*situated* on the second floor.'

'Smaller,' is an example of the Comparative Degree, which may be mentioned by anticipation.

10. A good example to bring out the distinction between 'all' and 'every.'

11. 'Several' is here the Indefinite Numeral. Refer back to No. 7.

12. 'Certain,' Indefinite Numeral.

'Swimming' is an example of a peculiar substitute for the Adjective, namely, the form of the Infinitive called the Gerund. The full expression is 'a bladder for swimming.' 'A swimming bladder' does not mean 'a bladder that swims.'

13. A sentence illustrating a peculiar distributive couple, 'the one—the other.' 'The other,' in this case, viewed by itself, may be considered an Ordinal Numeral, signifying the

second of two: the effect of the two phrases together is distributive.

16. Another case of the couple, 'one—other.' 'Short,' 'scanty,' Adjs. of Quantity in Mass or Bulk.

'Short' is an example of an Adjective in the predicate, 'fall' being here an incomplete verb.

'Abed' contracted from 'on bed,' must be parsed as the equivalent of an Adjective of Quality.

'When you are abed.' This is a case where the Indefinite Pronoun 'one' would be a more polite form of expression—'when one is abed.'

17. 'One' in this case has very little more force than the Indefinite Article 'a.'

'Horrible,' is an Adjective of Quality, the kind being—'pleasure and pain' (see THE ADVERB, p. 86.)

18. 'Narrow,' 'petty,' 'huge,' Quantity in Mass or Bulk.

20. An example of the Distributive couple, 'one—another.'

'Of a house,' is a prepositional phrase, serving the purpose of an Adjective, the full expression being—'belonging to a house.' 'A,' the indefinite article, in this case has the full force of the numeral 'one.' Compare above, No. 17

Exercise 10—(p. 71).

Adjectives Generally.

It is presumed that the teacher will have no difficulty in distinguishing Pronominal Adjectives, and Adjectives of Quantity; the following remarks, therefore, point rather to other distinctions.

1. 'Better,' 'guilty,' and 'innocent,' are Adjectives of Quality, Good and Evil.

'Better' is farther an example of a Comparative, and of an Adjective in the Predicate.

2. 'Blameless,' 'good,' Adjs. of Quality, Good and Evil: 'old,' Adj. of Quality, Time. It would be well now and again to ask the pupil how he knows whether a given Adjective is an Adjective of Quality. (See Grammar, p. 63, and above, q. 14).

'Good' is a co-ordinate Adjective: 'old' is the restrictive or specifying Adjective.

3. 'Foremost,' Quality, Space.

'The foremost man of all this world,' is a singular designation made up of significant names. The pupil might be asked whether there is any superfluous word in this expression. The 'all' might be dispensed with.

4. 'Holy,' 'heavenly,' Quality, Good and Evil.

5. 'Sloane,' a Noun used for an Adjective, a contracted form of expression for 'the Collection *that was made by* Sloane.'

'British,' being neither Pronominal nor Quantity, must be parsed as an Adj. of Quality. Of the leading classes given, it has most connection with that of Space.

6. 'Roast,' Adj. of Quality.

'The roast beef of Old England.' 'The,' 'roast,' and 'of Old England,' are all restrictive, all required to indicate the particular article intended.

'Of Old England,' is a prepositional phrase, used as an Adjective, equivalent to the Adjective clause '*that belongs to* Old England.'

'Old England's roast beef.' 'Old England's' is another equivalent for the same clause, a possessive case.

7. 'The choice and master spirits of his age.' The prepositional phrase 'of his age,' restricts the already limited class to one particular generation. 'Choice' is an Adj. of Quality: 'master,' a noun substitute for an Adjective, equivalent to 'masterly,' or to the clause 'that had the mastery.'

8. 'Anxious,' 'pensive,' Adjs. of Quality, sub-division—Pleasure and Pain (See ADVERB, p. 86). 'Secret,' Adj. of Quality. The pupil may here be reminded that the classes of Adjectives of Quality given in the Grammar are not exhaustive; and that the classes of Adverbs are also classes of Adjectives, and inversely.

9. 'Living in the country,' participial phrase, serving in place of an Adjective, equivalent to the clause 'that live.' 'Living' might be omitted, and thus the participial phrase would be contracted to a prepositional phrase. This illustrates how an Adverbial Phrase of Place, is by the omission of its verb, left alone as an Adjective Phrase. For a farther compression of the phrase, see below, No. 12.

'Town made' is a compressed participial phrase, from 'made in town.' 'Made' might be omitted, and then 'town' would stand alone, a noun used in place of an Adjective.

'*Retail* traders,' 'traders *that sell in retail,*' a Noun used for an Adjective.

'*The retail* traders *of the neighbourhood.*' All the three adjuncts are restrictive. 'Of the neighbourhood,' is a prepositional phrase, equivalent to the clause, '*that belong to* the neighbourhood.'

10. 'Whose birth beyond all question springs from great and glorious, though forgotten kings,' is an adjective clause, restricting 'boys.'

In such an expression as 'great and glorious Alexander,' —these Adjectives are co-ordinate; but here they restrict kings, narrow the whole class of kings to those possessing these attributes.

11. In 'mighty Nimrod,' 'mighty' (an Adj. of Quality) is co-ordinate, filling in the attributes of an individual already specified: but here it is used to restrict the class 'hunter.' 'Mighty hunters,' is a smaller class than 'hunters.'

12. '*Country* cousins,' '*town* friends.' Here we have a farther contraction of the participial phrase 'living in the country.' 'Country,' and 'town,' are parsed as Nouns used in place of Adjectives: and viewed as contractions from the clauses—'that live in the country,' and 'that live in the town.'

'Unwelcome,' Adj. of Quality, Pleasure and Pain.

13. Point out that the Predicate Adjective 'great' does not restrict 'these little things' in the subject, but 'things' understood in the predicate.

14. 'Pious,' Adj. of Quality, Good and Evil. 'Closing,' equivalent to 'when it closes,' a participle used as an Adjective.

15. 'This face of mine'—another instance of the predicate form of the possessive Adjective. The rule seems to be that this form is used wherever the Possessive Adjective is not followed by the noun it restricts.

'Deeper,' Adj. of Quality, Space, comparative degree.

16. 'Every' is more emphatic than 'all:' meaning 'all' taken separately, 'every' brings the statement home, as it were, to the individual.

'Upon this earth,' is a prepositional adjective phrase. We may suppose the omission of 'that lives.'

17. 'Sensible,' Adj. of Quality. 'Great,' 'that,' 'one,' 'twenty,' are easy cases.

18. 'Battled,' Adj. of Quality. [The proper Adjective is 'battlemented,' or 'embattled:' 'battled' is a poetic form.]

'Donjon,' one would suppose from the form to be a Noun used for an Adjective, restricting a more general designation in the word 'keep.' Really, however, 'donjon' and 'keep' are different names for the same thing.

'Loophole grates,' Noun used as Adjective, equivalent probably to the clause—'grates that were placed over loopholes.'

'Where captives weep,' an Adjective clause. This clause is co-ordinate, not restrictive: 'the loophole grates' indicates the place, and the clause separates a circumstance.

'Flanking,' parsed like 'closing' (14).

'That round it sweep,' Adjective clause, must be taken as co-ordinate, if we suppose the particular walls to be already denoted. In that case, 'which' is the proper relative.

19. 'High,' Adj. of Quality, Space.

'Midsummer,' Noun used as Adjective; 'midsummer pomps'='pomps that appear in midsummer.' Both 'high' and 'midsummer' are restrictive: without either we should not know the 'pomps' intended: 'high' points us to the splendours of the sky, and 'midsummer' to the skyey splendours of a particular time of year.

20. 'Mine,' predicate form.

'The heart *that can itself defend,*' Adjective clause, restrictive.

21. 'Loud,' Adj. of Quality, Sound.

'That spoke the vacant mind.' 'That' is the restrictive relative, and we may take the clause as specifying a particular kind of 'loud laugh.' Had the relative been 'which,' the meaning would have been that *every* loud laugh spoke the vacant mind, 'which' merely superadding a statement about something already specified.

'Vacant,' Adj. of Quality, Space.

22. 'Every,' more emphatic than 'all:' 'best,' superlative of 'good:' 'moderate,' Adj. of Quantity, Mass or Bulk: 'good,' Adj. of Quality, used as a Noun.

23. 'That try this mighty march,' Adjective clause, restrictive.

'Mighty,' must here be viewed as co-ordinate: 'this' sufficiently indicates the march intended, and 'mighty' is a superadded epithet, or simply an 'epithet,' strictly so called.

24 'Good' is here little more than an expletive for filling up the sound: 'fair' and 'foul,' Adjectives of Quality, Pleasure and Pain.

' Of fair and foul weather,' prepositional Adjective phrase, co-ordinate, equivalent to 'that contained both fair and foul weather.'

25. 'Northern,' Adj. of Quality, Space: 'sevenfold,' Definite Numeral, Multiplying: 'steadfast,' Adj. of Quality, Motion.

26. This is a complicated and difficult sentence to analyse and parse. 'Deep,' an Adjective in form (Quality, Space), is here properly an adverb of place. 'Shady,' Adj. of Quality, Colour. 'Far sunken from the healthy breath of morn,' a Participial Adjective phrase, restricting vale, indicating the kind of vale. 'Healthy,' Adj. of Quality. 'Far from the

fiery noon and eve's one star,' Prepositional Adjective phrase (*sunken* or *situated* being omitted): would have been restrictive or specifying had it come first, but coming when the nature of the vale has already been specified by the preceding clause, must be viewed as co-ordinate. 'Fiery,' Adjective of Quality, co-ordinate. 'Gray-haired,' Adj. of Quality, co-ordinate: would have been restrictive had there been several Saturns, and gray hairs distinctive of one of them. 'Quiet as a stone,' may be viewed either as an Adjective completion of the verb 'sat,' or as an Adverbial qualification, the Adjective 'quiet' being used as an Adverb. 'Quiet,' Adj. of Quality, Sound.

Here we have to do properly only with Adjectives: but it may be mentioned by anticipation that the three first lines are an Adverbial phrase of Place, indicating where Saturn sat.

27. 'Gold bound,' Participial Adjective phrase; co-ordinate —being unnecessary for the specifying of the brow, already denoted by the address; equivalent to the clause 'that art bound with gold.'

28. 'Additional,' Adj. of Quantity, Mass or Bulk. It is here restrictive: 'additional reputation' cannot be applied so widely as 'reputation.'

'Memorable,' Adj. of Quality, restrictive or co-ordinate according to the meaning intended. If the meaning is that Jerusalem sustained also sieges that are not memorable, and that it is the number and importance of the memorable ones that have made her famous, then memorable is restrictive, narrowing down the whole number of her sieges to those that are memorable. If, however, 'the number and importance *of her sieges*' alone would convey the intended meaning, then memorable is a co-ordinate epithet.

29. 'Stony,' Adj. of Quality, restrictive. 'Inhuman,' Adj. of Quality, Good and Evil; co-ordinate—'inhuman wretch' being as widely applicable as 'wretch.'

'Incapable of pity,' Participial Adjective phrase, co-ordinate, equivalent to 'who' (not *that*) 'is incapable of pity.'

'Void and empty' &c., another phrase of the same kind.

30. 'Attacks *in flank and rear,*' Prepositional Adjective phrase, restrictive, equivalent to 'attacks *that might be made* in flank and rear.'

'*The* Allies,' an instance of the particularising force of 'the,' *the* Allies that are concerned in our present history.

'Besieging,' Participial Adjective phrase, restrictive: 'the forces' alone would not be sufficient to denote the body intended.

'All,' though among the words of the predicate, really qualifies the subject.

'Upon the Chersonese,' a Prepositional Adjective phrase, used to complete the verb 'were.'

'Which was, &c.' is a clear instance of a co-ordinate Adjective clause, introduced by the proper relative 'which.'

31. 'Light,' 'busy,' 'peaceful,' Adjs. of Quality.

The two last lines form a co-ordinate participial phrase.

'Heaven's,' possessive case used as Adjective, equivalent to 'the best treasures *bestowed by* Heaven.'

32. 'The unphilosophical artists of the circus.' 'Unphilosophical' (Quality) is co-ordinate, 'of the circus' (Prepositional Adjective phrase) being sufficient to let us know the class of artists intended.

'Standing or dancing upon his horse's back,' is not an adjectival but an Adverbial Participial phrase.

'Which he is afterwards to receive on the sharpened point of a sword,' co-ordinate Adjective clause.

'Sharpened,' and 'of a sword,' are both restrictive. 'Sharpened,' a participle, equivalent to '*that has been* sharpened.'

The last clause—'connected with the most refined conclusions of science,' is restrictive. Only a portion of 'physical truths,' can be so designated.

THE VERB.

Answers to Questions (p. 80).

Q. 1. 'Shines,' 'break,' and 'hear' are called Verbs, because they affirm or predicate.

Q. 3. The test of a Verb is that it predicates. If 'water,' 'thunder,' 'house,' 'chair,' are ever used as the leading words in predication, then in such cases they must be parsed as Verbs. 'Water' is a Verb in the following sentence:—The girl *waters* the flowers. 'Thunder' in the following:—When Nature *thunders* in our opening ears. 'House' in the following:—They were comfortably *housed* and fed. 'Chair' in the following:—The successful candidate was *chaired* by his supporters.

Q. 5. Their arrival *created* a stir. The man *lifted* the boy on his shoulders. The wind *drives* the chaff before it. My friend *touched* my elbow. Their previous successes *encouraged* them.

Q. 6. Sentences with Transitive Verbs give the fullest meaning, because they give not only the subject and the action, but also the object of the action.

Q. 7. For this purpose we may use any of the sentences given in answer to Q. 5. A stir *was created* by their arrival. The boy *was lifted* by the man. The chaff *is driven* by the wind.

My elbow *was touched* by my friend. They *were encouraged* by their previous successes.

Q. 8. The leaf trembles; the wind raves; the old man talks; the child lisps; the music swells; the river flows; the drums beat; the heart throbs.

Q. 9. Besides those in the Grammar, the following are other cases that may be used for illustration:—sings a song—sings; paints a picture—paints; drives a horse—drives; hears a sound—hears.

Exercise 11—(p. 79).

The Verb.

1-4. 'Failed,' 'broke,' 'developes,' 'love,' are all Intransitive. 'Failed,' and 'broke,' express past time: 'developes,' and 'live,' express present time. The pupil may be asked to give instances where 'break' and 'develope' are used as Transitive Verbs: such as—The child broke the glass; Study developes the mind. When these Verbs are used as Intransitive, the subject is supposed to undergo the action of itself, the agent not being obvious.

'See' is here transitive.

'Do' (See Gram. p. 143) is what is called an Auxiliary Verb, rather helping to express the time of an action, than expressing any action itself.

5. 'Left' transitive; 'returned,' intransitive. The difficulty here is in the parsing of 'poor' and 'rich.' They must be viewed as Adjectives in co-ordination with the subject 'he,' and completing or adding to the meaning of the predicate Verbs 'left' and 'returned.'

'Left' is sometimes intransitive, as—he *left* yesterday.

'Returned' is sometimes transitive, as—Have you *returned* his umbrella?

6. 'Clean,' completes the meaning of 'sweep.' It may be parsed as an adjective used for an adverb, expressing the manner of the sweeping: but it is more correctly regarded as an adjective completion of the Verb, in co-ordination with the understood noun for the surface swept.

7. 'Whispered,' 'bleat,' intransitive. Here, as in No. 4, the verb 'do' is used as a pure auxiliary to express time.

8. 'Conquer,' intransitive, the object being omitted. This is an opportunity for repeating how it is that Transitive Verbs pass into Intransitive.

9. 'Is,' Verb of Incomplete Predication, completed by the phrase 'the greatest of our senses.'

'See' being used transitively, while 'hear' is used intransitively, there is thus another opportunity for enforcing the change from Transitive to Intransitive.

'Loud,' and 'close,' are completions of 'are,' restricting 'sounds' understood in the predicate.

10. 'Eat,' 'drink,' intransitives formed by the omission of their objects. 'Die' is used only in an intransitive sense.

11. 'Endeavours,' a Transitive Verb, having for its object not a simple noun, but the whole infinitive phrase—'to substitute education for coercion.

'Deserves,' is usually a Transitive Verb. Here it seems to have no object, 'well' being an adverb, and as such expressing manner. But though 'well' is an adverb in form, it is here really used as a noun, and as such is the object of 'deserves.'

12. 'Happy,' a predicate adjective, completion of 'were' understood, restricting 'times' understood.

'Styled,' Verb of Incomplete Predication, completed by the noun 'fathers' with its adjunct 'of families.'

13. 'As high as the roof of a cathedral (is),' an adjective (high) qualified by an adverbial clause, is here the completion of 'are.'

In No. 6, 'sweep' is intransitive by the omission of its object: here 'sweeps' is purely intransitive, never being used transitively in this sense.

'Roaring' cannot here be said to express the manner of the 'sweep,' for in that case it would have been parsed as a participle used for an adverb. It rather adds an independent circumstance to the predicate, and must be viewed as an adjective completion.

'Beats,' intransitive. It is usually a Transitive Verb, but here the object is omitted, the action being of much more importance than the object. 'Against the pillars' is here an adverbial phrase, expressing the place where the beating action occurs.

'Paved with ruddy marble,' completion of the Incomplete Verb 'seems,' a participial adjective phrase.

'Can' is sometimes parsed as an Auxiliary Verb, serving merely to express circumstance, the circumstance of potentiality, the action being viewed as a possible action. It is, however, more correct to view it as a Verb of Incomplete Predication, having the infinitive '(to) come in,' as its completion.

'Placid,' adjective completion of 'is.'

14. 'Wax,' and 'prove,' are here incomplete predicates, of which the adjectives 'poor' and 'unkind' are the completions.

15. 'Lighted,' intransitive, contracted from alighted.

'Seemed to touch,' a Verb of incomplete predication, completed by the infinitive of a Transitive Verb.

'Decorating' and 'cheering,' participles of Transitive Verbs. The whole clause that they introduce is a participial adjective phrase to 'her.'

'Began to move,' Verb of incomplete predication, completed by the infinitive of an Intransitive Verb.

'Which she hardly seemed to touch,' is a good instance of a co-ordinate adjective clause.

16. The completion of 'is,' in this case, is the prepositional phrase 'for thee.'

'Ascends,' 'sings,' intransitive.

'Tunes,' 'elevates,' 'pours,' 'swells,' are all transitive.

THE ADVERB.

Answers to Questions (p. 90).

Q. 1. The Adjective and the Adverb agree in being adjuncts, and not principal words in the sentence. They differ in the parts of speech that they are adjuncts to: the Adjective is an adjunct of the Noun, the Adverb of the Verb, the Adjective, or another Adverb. The answer may be briefly tabulated as follows :—

The ADVERB—

Agrees with the ADJECTIVE—

In being an Adjunct, not a principal word.

Differs from the Adjective—

In the Parts of Speech whose meaning it modifies.

Q. 2. The Adverb expresses modes of actions :—walking *lazily, rapidly, steadily;* looking *eagerly, vacantly, steadfastly;* working *regularly, fitfully, industriously;* sailing *swiftly, smoothly, slowly.*

Q. 3. The great nicety in regard to 'where,' 'whence,' and 'whither,' is their use as cases of pronouns. Generally, and as adverbs proper, they signify 'in which place,' 'from which place,' and 'to which place:' but when they refer back to a Noun, as in the following expressions—'the district where we live,' 'the country whence he came,' 'the land whither thou goest,' they are equivalent to 'in which,' 'from which,' and 'to which,' a case of the relative, or a preposition with the relative.

Q. 11. This is the only other question that cannot be answered by a repetition or a simple modification of the text.

Most of the Adjectives of Quality enumerated at p. 64 (Gram.) may be transformed into Adverbs by adding 'ly.' Here, therefore we need notice only the exceptions.

Time.—The Adverb corresponding to 'following' is formed from a synonymous word—subsequent; 'subsequently.'

The Adverb corresponding to 'future' is 'hereafter.'

The Adverb corresponding to 'contemporary' is taken from another form of the Adjective—contemporaneous; 'contemporaneously.'

'Approaching.' The corresponding Adverb is 'approximately,' from the Latin form of the Adjective.

'Bygone'—'in former days.'

'Ancient.' 'Anciently' is used, but 'in old times' is most common.

'Modern,' 'now-a-days.'

'Young'—'youthfully,' from another form of the Adjective.

'Early' is itself used as an Adverb.

Space.—'Expanded,'—'expansively,' from another form of the Adjective.

'Long,' is used as an Adverb without change of form.

'Straight.' In the meaning of 'not crooked,' the Adverb is 'straightly.' 'Straight' is used as an Adverb in the sense of 'immediately,' 'directly.'

The Adverbs most nearly corresponding to 'level' and 'plane' are 'evenly,' and 'flatly.'

'Hanging,' 'pendently.'

'Inclined,' 'obliquely.'

'Crossed,' 'across.'

'Outer,' 'inner'—'out,' 'in.' 'Outerly' is sometimes used.

'Covered' and 'bare' have no immediately corresponding

Adverbs. 'Covertly' means 'secretly;' 'barely,' with 'difficulty.'

'Foremost' and 'hindermost,' like 'first' and 'last' are Adverbs as well as Adjectives.

Form.—'Sloped,' 'bent,' 'columnar,' 'concave,' have no immediately corresponding Adverbs. We have, however, 'concavously.'

Motion.—'Movingly' means pathetically. There are no Adverbs immediately corresponding to 'sailing,' 'advancing,' 'receding,' 'admitting,' 'excluding,' 'rising,' 'falling,' 'turning,' 'vibrating.'

Solidity.—The Adjectives corresponding to 'polished' are 'smoothly,' 'politely;' to 'frozen,' 'frostily,' 'chilly.'

Fluidity.—'Fluid,' 'fluently:' 'molten,' 'meltingly.'

'Watery,' 'wet,' 'moist,' 'bubbling,' 'purling,' have no corresponding Adverbs.

Colour.—'Coloured,' and the various adjective names of the colours have no corresponding Adverbs.

Good and Evil.—All these have corresponding Adverbs. The reason is that, they all have a reference to action: unless the meaning of an Adjective can be turned so as to express the manner of an action, the Adjective cannot be converted into an Adverb.

The teacher should make much of the foregoing exercise. It is simple, and will make the pupils think and ransack their dictionaries.

Exercise 12 (p. 88.)

The Adverb.

1. 'By Columbus,' adverbial phrase of *Agency* (which may be considered a mode of Cause and Effect), qualifying 'was discovered.'

'In the year 1492,' adverbial phrase of time.

2. 'By studying economy,' adverbial phrase of *Means* (Cause and Effect), qualifying 'live like a lord.'

'Like a lord,' is an Adjective completion of the incomplete verb 'live.'

3. 'Merrily,' adverb of Manner, *Pleasure and Pain.*

'As a lark' (sings) 'on a spring morning,' an adverbial clause of Degree or Comparison, qualifying 'merrily.'

'On a spring morning,' phrase of Time, qualifying 'sings.'

4. 'To breakfast,' adv. phrase of *Purpose* (Cause), qualifying 'came down.'

'Every morning,' adv. phrase of time, noun and adjective with preposition 'on' omitted, qualifying 'came down.'

'In that summer visit of the year 1638,' adv. phrase of time.

'Of the year 1638,' is an adjective phrase, restricting 'summer visit.'

5. 'Only,' adv. of Degree.

'Willingly,' adv. of Manner, *Pleasure and Pain.*

'With their whole strength,' adv. phrase of degree.

'At the general burden,' adv. phrase of Place, *metaphorical.*

6. 'Cheerfully,' adv. of Manner, *Pleasure and Pain.*

'With despatch,' adv. phrase of Time.

7. 'Half-a-league,' noun used as adverb, adverbial phrase of Measure with preposition 'for,' or 'through' omitted.

'Onward,' adverb of Place, *Motion to.*

8. 'To right of them,' 'to left of them,' adverbial phrases of Place, *Relative Position (Rest in).* This is the proper parsing, if the phrases are taken as qualifying the verbs understood 'volleyed and thundered:' they may also be regarded as prepositional adjective phrases co-ordinate with 'cannon.'

9. 'Somewhere,' adv. of Place, *Rest in:* 'somehow,' adv. of Manner: 'by some beings,' adv. phrase of *Agency* (Cause and Effect). All these qualify the action of the sentence, which is not expressed. The completion of the sentence is—'a battle was travelling through all its stages;' and these adverbs qualify 'was travelling.'

The corresponding adverbs 'where' (Place), 'how' (Manner) and 'by whom' (Agency), also qualify 'was travelling,' but in a somewhat different connection. The full expression of the subordinate clauses is—'I know not where *it was travelling through all its stages,*' 'I knew not how &c.,' 'I knew not by whom &c.,' and the adverbs qualify the understood Verb.

10. 'Down,' adv. of Place, *Motion to*, qual. 'go.' 'Above,' 'below,' advs. of Place, *Relative Position* (Rest in), qualifying 'resting,' or 'placed' understood.

11. 'In struggles' is here probably not to be regarded as an adverbial phrase expressing the manner of the awaking, but as an adjective phrase, complement of the incomplete verb 'awoke,' expressing the state of the person when awaking.

'Aloud,' adv. of Manner, *Sound.*

'No more,' adverbial phrase of Time, *Duration in Future Time*, equivalent to 'never in time to come,' and contracted from the full phrase 'during no more time.'

12. 'On the morrow,' adv. phrase of Time, *Future*, qual. 'leave.'

'As my hopes have flown before,' adv. clause of *Comparison*, qual. whole of preceding expression.

13. 'Presently,' adv. of Time, *Future*, qual. 'grew stronger' (incomplete verb with comparative adjective complement).

'No longer,' adv. phrase of Time, *Duration*, full expression —'for no longer time,' qual. 'hesitating.'

'Truly,' adv. of Certainty.

14. 'Shoreward,' adv. of Place, *Motion to*.

'Soon,' adv. of Time, *Duration*. The two adverbs qualify 'roll.'

15. 'Slowly,' adv. of Time, *Duration*.

'Sadly,' adv. of Manner, *Pleasure and Pain*. 'Down,' adv. of Place, *Motion to*. 'From the field of his fame fresh and gory,' is a co-ordinate adjective phrase to 'him.' If we analyse the phrase by itself, we must suppose such a verb as 'borne,' or 'taken,' which is completed by the adjectives 'fresh and gory,' and adverbially qualified by the phrase 'from the field of his fame'—adverbial phrase of place, *Motion from*.

16. 'Many a time, adv. phrase of Time, *Repetition*: 'oft,' adv. of Time, *Repetition*: 'in the Rialto,' adv. phrase of Place, *Rest in*. All qualify the verb of the sentence, stating the circumstances of the action.

17. 'As often happens,' Adv. phrase of Time, expressing *Degree of Repetition*. It may be said to be an Adv. of Degree or an Adv. of Time: it expresses *degree of time*. It qualifies the whole assertion.

'Half-way,' adv. of Place, *Rest in*.

18. 'In the first place,' adv. phrase of Place, metaphorical: it qualifies the whole predicate.

'Almost,' adv. of Degree, qual. 'exclusively.'

'Exclusively,' adv. of Manner, expressing originally the idea of *Motion*.

19. 'Necessarily,' adv. of Certainty: 'from the very mode and nature of his existence,' adv. phrase of Cause: 'to all intents,' adv. of Degree. All these qualify the predicate 'is a speculative being.'

20. 'There.' This is the peculiar idiom of 'there' mentioned in Grammar, p. 82. In such cases it may be called an 'Expletive,' or 'filling-out' word, serving merely as a temporary stop-gap till the subject of the verb is brought up.

'Half,' adv. of Measure.

'So,' adv. of Comparison.

'In life,' Adverbial phrase of Place, qual. 'existing,' or some such word, understood—'nothing existing (or that exists) in life is half so sweet as, &c.' If we omit all reference to the understood verb, 'in life' must be taken as an adjective phrase restricting 'thing.'

'As Love's young dream' (is), adverbial clause of Comparison.

21. 'Some day,' adv. phrase of Indefinite Time, with preposition 'on' omitted. 'Day' may be parsed as a Noun used for an Adverb.

'Not yet,' adv. of Future Time.

22. 'Still,' adjective completion of 'lay.' 'Until I was within a hundred yards of him,' adv. clause of Time, *Future* (to the predicate 'lay still').

Within a hundred yards of him,' here appears as an adjective completion (prepositional phrase) of the verb 'was:' but in strict sense it is an adverbial phrase qualifying some such verb as 'situated,' 'stationed,' or 'standing,' understood.

'Slowly,' adv. of Manner, *Motion.*

'On his fin-like legs,' adv. phrase of Manner, *Motion.*

'Towards the river,' adv. phrase of Place, *Motion to.*

'Askance,' adverb of Manner, *Motion.*
'At me,' adv. phrase of Place, *metaphorical: Direction.*

23. 'Steadfastly,' adv. of Manner, *Motion.*
'On the face that was dead,' adv. phrase of Place, *Direction.*
'Bitterly,' adv. of Manner, *Pleasure and Pain.*

24. 'At the close of the day,' adverbial phrase of Time: 'when the hamlet is still,' adv. clause of Time.

25. Adverbial phrases of Manner.

26. 'After dinner,' adv. phrase of Time. 'In his chair,' adv. phrase of Place.

'Idle,' is an adjective completion of 'sat:' the adv. phrases qualify the predicate 'sat idle.'

'Ruddy, fat, and fair,' must be treated as co-ordinate adjectives, superadding information, and doing nothing to restrict.

27. 'Since last we met,' adv. clause of Time, *Past.* 'Last,' is here used as an Adverb of Degree or Measure of Time. The full expression is 'since the last time when we met.'

The case illustrates how Prepositions pass into Conjunctions; see Grammar, p. 104.

'Again,' adv. of Time, *Repetition.*

''Tis years,' is a curious idiomatic expression. 'Years' is a noun completion of 'is,' and though plural in form, is treated as a singular expression for a period of time.

28. 'Darkly,' adv. of Manner, *Colour*: 'deeply,' adv. of Degree: 'beautifully' adv. of Manner, *Pleasure and Pain.* All these qualify the adjective 'blue,' and in such a position are all adverbs of Degree, expressing a degree of the colour 'blue.'

'Somewhere,' adv. of Place, indefinite.

'About the sky,' adverb of Place, *metaphorical*, expressing the subject or *topic*.

29. 'A very long way,' adv. phrase of Degree in Place, preposition 'for' omitted. 'Very' is an adv. of Degree: 'a long way,' without the 'very,' would have been a phrase of degree.

30. 'Ten times,' adv. phrase of Degree in Time, preposition 'for' omitted.

31. 'Of her softest mould,' adv. phrase of *Material* (Cause and Effect), expressing also Degree.

'With tender passions,' adv. phrase of *Instrument* (Cause and Effect).

'Even,' adv. of Degree.

'Below my weak sex,' adv. phrase of Place, *Relative Position (Rest in)*.

32. 'Where,' interrogative adverb of Place, *Rest in*. 'Home,' noun used as Adverb, adverbial phrase with preposition 'to' omitted.

33. 'Beneath this cold slab,' 'in the chapel,' 'in the Abbey,' adv. phrases of Place, *Rest in*.

'Now,' adv. of Time, *Present*.

34. 'Soundly,' adv. of Manner: 'very,' adv. of Degree.

'Much,' and 'better,' usually adjectives, are here both adverbs. 'Composed' is the adjective completion of 'waked.'

'Than I had ever been before,' adv. clause of Comparison.

'Ever,' adv. of Time, *Indefinite*. 'Before,' adv. of Time, *Past*.

'Now,' adv. of Time, *Present*. 'Sedately,' adv. of Manner.

'Upon the utmost debate with myself,' adverbial phrase of Cause.

'So,' adv. of Comparison: 'exceeding,' adjective improperly used as adverb, Degree.

'No farther from the mainland than as I had seen,' adv. phrase of Place. 'Than as I had seen,' adv. clause of Comparison, 'than' being the leading word of comparison, 'as' not being concerned in the comparison, but serving simply as an adverb of Manner.

'Entirely,' Adv. of Degree.

'So entirely as I might imagine,' Adv. clause of Comparison.

35. 'First,' adv. of Place, *Relative Position.*

'As he flew,' adv. clause of Time. 'As' has here no meaning of Comparison.

'A moment,' noun used as adverb, or adverbial phrase of Time, with the preposition 'for' omitted.

'Upon his way,' adv. phrase of Place.

'If his eyes were good,' adv. clause of *Condition* (Cause and Effect), qualifying the whole of the principal clause.

'By night,' adv. phrase of Time.

'Every day,' adv. phrase of Time, *Repetition,* with preposition 'on' omitted.

36. 'Deep,' adjective used by poetical license for adverb 'deeply,' adv. of Degree.

'O'er our heads,' adv. phrase of Place, *Relative Position.*

'Imminent,' is not an adjective used for an adverb, but an adjective complement of the verb 'hung.'

'With imperious gloom,' adv. phrase of Manner, *Colour.*

37. 'With such a companion,' adv. phrase of Manner, qual. 'to tend.' 'As—as a feather' (is light), adv. clause of Comparison, qualifying 'was light.'

'So—as never was known,' adv. clause of Comparison, qualifying 'am grown easy.'

'Strangely,' adv. of Manner.

'Up' and 'down,' in 'rise up' and 'lie down,' are strictly Adverbs, expressing the direction of the action; but they are so often used in the same connection that they must almost be regarded as parts of the Verb, or as constituting Compound Verbs.

THE PREPOSITION.

Answers to Questions—(p. 101).

Q. 1. The Preposition is called a word of *relation* because it cannot stand by itself as Subject, Predicate, or Adjunct of Subject or of Predicate, but is used simply to *relate* or connect other words, so as to form Adjuncts. The words related by the Preposition are chiefly Verbs and Nouns.

Such words as 'street,' 'rattles,' 'stony,' 'loudly,' convey a certain meaning in themselves, may stand by themselves among the four principal Parts of a Sentence: but such words as 'to,' 'with,' 'beneath,' cannot stand by themselves among the four leading Parts, but can appear only as parts of those parts, as part*icles*, or little parts. These particles are employed in the making up of adjuncts, serving chiefly, as has been seen, to introduce adverbial phrases, or phrases that, once adverbial, have by contraction become apparently adjectival.

As adverbial phrases always qualify verbs, expressed or understood, and consist of a preposition and a noun (with or without adjuncts), the function of the Preposition may be said to be *relating*, or attaching, or hooking, or linking on, nouns to verbs.

Q. 2. Pronouns and Conjunctions are also words of relation. The Pronoun relates in a different way. It is not, like the Preposition, incapable of standing by itself as one of the four great Parts of a Sentence; it may stand in every place open to the Noun: but it has no meaning by itself; it relates or refers to some other part of speech. The Conjunction, as will be seen, relates in a way similar to the Preposition.

Q. 4. This question cannot be fully understood without anticipating the idea that a clause may stand in place of a Noun. In such sentences as—'He said *that he would do it;*' 'I have done *what I promised*'—'that he would do it,' and 'what I promised,' being the objects of the transitive verbs 'said' and 'done,' are regarded as standing in place of Nouns, and spoken of as Noun Clauses; just as clauses standing in place of Adjectives and Adverbs are called Adjective Clauses and Adverbial Clauses. In such clauses as—'Since *I left home,*' 'before *I came here,*' 'after *he met me,*'—'I left home,' 'I came here,' and 'he met me,' may be regarded as Noun Clauses coming after 'since,' 'before,' and 'after,' in which view 'since,' 'before,' and 'after,' are Prepositions. But this nice analysis is not attended to; and 'since,' 'before,' and 'after,' are in such cases called Conjunctions. The analysis is, however, useful as showing one probable origin of Conjunctions.

Q. 8. Other phrases besides those mentioned at this point in the text are such as—in case of, in the event of, from a regard to, in respect of, by means of, through the instrumentality of, in accordance with.

Q. 12. 'The heat of the fire,' *Attributive* meaning of 'of:' the heat is not a part or division of the fire, but an attribute or quality of the fire.

'The wing of the butterfly,' *Partitive* meaning: the wing

is a part of the animal. In 'the beauty of the butterfly,' 'of' is *Attributive.*

'The love of the child,' *Reference* meaning. The reference may be either *from* the child or *to* the child: the meaning may be either 'the love felt by *(proceeding from)* the child to some person,' or the love *directed towards* the child by some person.

Q. 18. Even the prepositions of *Rest in a Place*, have a tacit reference to *direction* of previous movement. 'In' implies movement from some station regarded as 'out:' 'on' implies movement from a station regarded as 'off:' and similarly 'at,' 'near,' and 'by,' imply movements from opposed situations.

Q. 20. 'By,' 'through,' and 'with,' are all primarily Prepositions of Place.

In giving the different meanings of a Preposition or the sub-divisions of a class, frequent use should be made of the black board.

In exercising on the Prepositions, the teacher will find abundance of examples in the Exercises on the Adjective and the Adverb, **Exercises** 8, 9, 10, 12.

THE CONJUNCTION.

Answers to Questions—(p. 112).

Q. 1. Conjunctions and Prepositions *agree* in being words of relation: *differ* in the mode of their relation, Prepositions relating one part of speech to another in the same sentence, Conjunctions relating one sentence to another.

Q. 3. When we wish to know, in a given case, whether a word is an Adverb or a Conjunction, we must look to the purpose that it serves. If it modifies the meaning of a Verb, then it is an Adverb: if it joins two sentences together, then it is a Conjunction. Take, for example, the sentence—'He should have acted *otherwise*.' Here 'otherwise' qualifies the verb 'acted,' and is parsed as an Adverb. Take, again, the sentence—'He did not let me know that he was here; *otherwise* I should have gone and seen him.' Here 'otherwise' connects two sentences, and is a Conjunction.

Q. 4. The change of a word from Preposition to Conjunction is a somewhat difficult idea (see before, p. 74). To bring it fully out, the teacher should insist chiefly that the sentence introduced by the Conjunction may be regarded as a substitute for a Noun, and the Conjunction as a preposition relating that Noun Sentence or Clause to a verb.

Q. 7. '*If he had not missed his opportunity*, he might now have been a prosperous man.'

'They succeeded in business, *because their character inspired confidence.*'

'John has been confined to bed *since he met with that accident.*'

See also Exercise 14.

Q. 8. All the sentences in Exercise 13, are examples of Co-ordinate Sentences.

Q. 9. A small amount of dependence exists between sentences connected by 'and.' 'I went *and saw him* —the seeing of him is to some extent dependent upon the going, and the going upon the seeing. There always is a certain connection between two facts united by a Conjunction in statement. But in the sentence 'I went *in order that I might see him,*' the degree of dependence is much greater. In the first case, each clause states an actual fact, and the two are co-ordinate: in the second case, the one clause states an actual fact, and the other states a possibility depending upon that fact without saying whether it actually took place. In the one case you have two *co-ordinate* statements of fact; in the other a statement of fact and a *sub-ordinate* possibility. These are the two extremes.

Examples of 'either—or' lie between the two. 'Either you (must go) or I must go.' Here we have two co-ordinate dependencies, my going being dependent upon your going, and your going upon my going. The one fact is not so absolutely subordinated to the other as in the sentence—'I went in order that I might see him;' nor so much independent of the other as in the sentence—'I went and saw him.'

Q. 14. 'Also,' 'likewise,' and 'as well as,' have a certain meaning of comparison, as well as of cumulation or addition.

Exercise 13—(p. 108).

Co-ordinating Conjunctions.

There is no difficulty in this exercise, nor in the following: still, it may be convenient for the teacher to have a list beside him.

1. 'And,' co-ordinating, cumulative.

2. 'Else,' co-ordinating, adversative, exclusive.

3. 'Still,' co-ordinating, adversative, arrestive.

4. 'Only,' co-ordinating, adversative, arrestive.

5. 'However,' co-ordinating, adversative, arrestive.

6. 'But,' co-ordinating, adversative, arrestive.
'Or,' co-ordinating, adversative, alternative. The full expression would be :—'it takes the colour of the glass *that giveth the reflection*, or *it takes the colour of the* body that giveth the reflection.'

7. 'Either—or,' co-ordinating, adversative, alternative. Full expression—'A man's nature runs either to herbs or *it runs* to weeds.'

8. 'Yet,' co-ordinating, adversative, arrestive.
In the expression—'were those virtues more mature,' there is an omission of the conjunction 'if,' Subordinating, Condition.

9. 'And,' co-ordinating, cumulative: 'also,' co-ordinating, cumulative.

10. 'But,' co-ordinating, adversative, arrestive.
'For all that,' phrase, co-ordinating, adversative, arrestive.

11. 'Wherefore,' co-ordinating, illative.

12. 'Thus,' co-ordinating, illative: 'not only—but,' co-ordinating, cumulative.

13. 'Yet,' co-ordinating, adversative, arrestive.

14. 'So—that,' co-ordinating, illative.

15. 'Otherwise,' co-ordinating, adversative, exclusive.

16. 'Consequently,' co-ordinating, illative.

17. 'But,' co-ordinating, adversative, arrestive.

18. 'Nor,' co-ordinating, adversative, alternative. Full expression—'nor yet *was he* beside the rill, nor *was he* up the lawn, &c.'

'Yet' is here not a Conjunction, but an Adverb of Time, qualifying the predicate 'was beside the rill.' This is also a good sentence for Prepositions.

19. 'But then,' co-ordinating, adversative, arrestive. 'Then' has no illative force here.

20. 'Not only—but,' 'not only—but also,' co-ordinating, cumulative.

21. 'Therefore,' co-ordinating, illative. The full expression of this sentence would be—'There still remain for him cares, and *there still remain for him* duties, and, therefore, *there still remain for him* hopes.'

22. 'Whether—or,' co-ordinating, adversative, alternative.

23. 'As well as,' co-ordinating, cumulative.

24. 'Partly—partly,' co-ordinating, cumulative.

'Because,' and 'that,' are Subordinating Conjunctions of Reason.

25. 'Nevertheless,' co-ordinating, adversative, arrestive.

26. 'Accordingly,' co-ordinating, illative.

27. 'First—then,' co-ordinating, cumulative.

28. 'So—that,' co-ordinating, illative.

29. 'At the same time,' co-ordinating phrase, arrestive.

Exercise 14—(p. 110).

Conjunctions generally.

1. 'As—as,' subordinating, end or purpose. 'Or,' co-ordinating, adversative, alternative: full expression—'as a robe *is fit for a race* or a mantle, &c.'

2. 'If,' subordinating, condition.

3. 'Notwithstanding,' subordinating, condition.

4. 'Unless,' subordinating, condition.

5. 'So as,' subordinating, end or purpose.

6. 'As if,' subordinating, condition.

7. 'Then,' co-ordinating, illative: 'since,' subordinating, cause.

8. 'Lest,' subordinating, end or purpose.

9. 'Supposing that,' subordinating, condition: 'then,' co-ordinating, illative—elliptical for 'what *would happen* then?'

10. 'If not,' subordinating, condition. 'He was' is omitted in the conditional clause.

11. Farther example of 'if.'

12. 'That,' subordinating, end or purpose.

13. For,' subordinating, reason.

14. 'And,' co-ordinating, cumulative: 'as,' subordinating, time.

15. 'If,' subordinating, condition.

16. 'Though,' subordinating, condition.

17. 'Because,' subordinating, reason.

18. 'When,' 'while,' 'as,' subordinating, time.

19. 'Except,' subordinating, condition.

20. 'Nor,' co-ordinating, adversative, alternative: 'albeit, subordinating, condition—' he was,' understood.

21. 'When,' subordinating, time: 'but,' co-ordinating, adversative, arrestive.

INFLECTION:

Inflection for Gender.

Answers to Questions—(p. 116.)

Q. 2. The employing of different words to distinguish sex is not, strictly speaking, a process of Inflection, which is a change made in the termination of a word.

The black-board should be used to give emphasis to the three principal ways of distinguishing Gender. Some such skeleton as this may be sufficient:—

Gender is distinguished—

I. By *different words:* as—father, mother

II. By *prefixes:* as—he-wolf, she-wolf.

III. By *suffixes:* as—priest, priestess.

Q. 6. Enemy—*common:* prophet—*masculine:* author—*masculine:* Time—*masculine:* Mercy—*feminine:* vixen—*feminine:* breath—*neuter:* snow—*neuter:* wolf—*common:* tiger—*masculine:* salmon—*common.*

Q. 7. These may be written on the black-board in column, thus:—

Mas.	*Fem.*	*Mas.*	*Fem.*
Earl	Countess	He-bear	She-bear
Duke	Duchess	Lion	Lioness
Marquis	Marchioness	Instructor	Instructress
Traitor	Traitress	Testator	Testatrix
Director	Directrix		

Inflection for Number.

Answers to Questions—(p. 121).

These questions also present no difficulty. The teacher's chief care in enforcing the various rules and remarks about the formation of the plural should be first to vary the statement, next to detach passages relating to the same point, and tabulate them under heads.

Sections 1-5 deal with the various forms of the plural inflection: sections 6-11 contain miscellaneous remarks. When the question is put—'What are the various modes of forming the plural?' the answer lies in sections 1-5.

The various modes of forming the plural may be tabulated as follows:—

Various Forms of Plural Inflection.

I. *Plurals in 's'—General rule.*—The Plural is generally formed by adding *s* to the Singular.

Various Modes of Plural in 's.' 1. *After sharp Mutes.* When the Noun ends in a sharp mute [*p, f, t, th* (in *th*in), *k*], the 's' has its sharp sound (*s*ea).

2. *After flat mutes.* When the Noun ends in a flat mute [*b, v, d, th* (in *the*), *g*], in a liquid (*m, n, l, r*), or in a vowel, the 's' has its flat sound *z*.

3. *After sibilants.* When the Noun ends in a sibilant or hissing sound (*s, z, sh, ch, x*), 'es' is added instead of 's.'

Plurals of nouns ending in 'o,' and of nouns ending in 'y,' preceded by a consonant, spell with 'es' instead of 's,' but pronounce simply with the *z* sound of 's,' according to Rule 2, for nouns ending in a vowel.

4. *Exception after 'f' or 'fe.'*—Nouns of Anglo-Saxon origin ending in 'f' or 'fe' preceded by a long vowel, or by 'l,' change the 'f' into 'v.'

Here also the spelling is in 'es;' and, 'v' being a flat mute, 's' sounds *z*.

II. *Obsolete Plurals.* A small number of Nouns form their plurals by obsolete modes of inflection.

1. By adding 'en' to the singular.
2. By adding 'ry' to the singular.
3. By changing the vowel of the singular.

III. *Plurals uniform with the Singular.* Some Nouns have the same form in both numbers.

IV. *Foreign Plurals.* Many words borrowed from other languages retain their original plurals.

With such a skeleton as the above before him, the teacher will awaken his pupils to the meaning and mutual relation of the various rules for forming the plural, by asking such questions as—"What are the various modes of the Plural in 's'?" "What is the sound of *s* after a flat mute?" "Does the general rule hold after sibilants?" "Do all nouns ending in sharp mutes take sharp 's' in the plural [pointing to 'f' in Rule 4]?" "Enumerate the obsolete modes of forming the plural"—and such-like.

Q. 2. The only classes of nouns that conform strictly to the general rule for forming the plural, are nouns ending in mutes, sharp or flat. The classes that do not conform strictly are nouns ending in sibilants, Anglo-Saxon nouns in 'f' preceded by a long vowel or by 'l,' and nouns borrowed directly from other languages. Besides these non-conforming 'classes,' there are various non-conforming individuals, that prefer to form the plural by obsolete modes, or to retain the same form in both numbers.

Q. 3. 'Cargoes' and 'beauties' are not an exception to the general rule in so far as pronunciation is concerned. They are pronounced exactly as if they formed the plural by adding 's' to the singular, the 's' having its sound of *z* after the vowel termination.

Q. 5. Bin, bins (z); chair, chairs (z); church, churches; street, streets; child, children; grotto, grottoes (z); staff, staffs or staves (z); stuff, stuffs; handkerchief, handkerchiefs; window, windows (z); ally, allies (z); spray, sprays (z); aviary, aviaries (z); wreath, wreaths.

Q. 8. Species, species; seraph, seraphim; criterion, criteria; formula, formulæ; focus, foci; bandit, banditti; virtuoso, virtuosi; Sir, Messieurs; Madam, Mesdames; larva, larvæ.

These plurals are irregular in English, as being borrowed from foreign languages, and retaining their original forms.

'Seraph,' 'formula,' and 'bandit,' take also the regular English plural in 'o:' seraphs, formulas (z), bandits.

The pupils may be asked whether the 'p' in these plurals sounds sharp *s* or *z*.

Q. 12. A noun of Material has no plural, because it is a name for the whole body of one kind of material all put together, not a name for separate individual objects. When used for separate parts or pieces of any one material, it becomes a general noun, and takes a plural (see Gram. p. 36).

Similarly with Abstract nouns. An Abstract noun is not a name for separate individuals, but for the resemblance that they bear to one another, and so is naturally singular. When the Abstract noun is used for more than one resemblance or agreement, it becomes a General noun, and takes a plural. (See Gram. p. 37).

The Questions on INFLECTION FOR CASE, on the INFLECTION OF PRONOUNS, and on the INFLECTION OF ADJECTIVES, need no special explanation.

Exercise 15—(p. 128).

Inflection of Nouns, Pronouns, Adjectives, and Adverbs.

In parsing for Inflection, the pupil should be trained to notice only words that are really inflected. Gender, Number, Case, or Degree, should not be remarked upon unless in words that are inflected to express such meanings. The singular number has no inflection, and need not be alluded to when the parsing is for inflection alone: and similarly with the nominative and the objective cases in nouns, and the positive degree in adjectives and in adverbs. The feminine gender, the plural number, the possessive case, and the comparative and superlative degrees, are the chief things to look out for.

When a sentence is taken up for examination, the pupils may be asked first of all to point out what words in the sentence are inflected, not beginning to specify the inflections until all the inflected words have been singled out.

1. In this sentence the only inflected word that we have to remark upon is 'hers,' the possessive case of the feminine of the third personal pronoun. In answer to the direction—Parse 'hers' for Inflection, the pupil may be expected to give some such answer as—'Hers,' demonstrative pronoun, inflected for Gender, Number, and Case; feminine gender, singular number, possessive case. In calling the word a pronoun, we really go beyond parsing for Inflection, and

parse for Parts of Speech: but at this stage it may be well not to insist upon such a nicety.

'Is' is also an inflected word, but being a verb it does not come under our notice at this stage. It is inflected for Number, Person, Tense or Time, and Mood.

2. The inflected words are 'it' and 'its.'—'It,' demonstrative pronoun, inflected for Gender and Number; neuter gender, singular number. 'Its,' third personal pronoun, inflected for Gender, Number, and Case; neuter gender, singular number, possessive case.

3. The inflected words are 'he,' 'others,' 'him,' 'his,' 'who.'—'He,' demonstrative pronoun, inflected for Gender, Number, and Case; masculine gender, singular number, nominative case. 'Him,' the same, objective case. 'His,' the same, possessive case. 'Others,' indefinite pronoun, inflected for Number; plural number. 'Who,' relative pronoun, inflected for Case; nominative case.

4. 'She,' 'her,' demonstrative pronoun, inflected for Gender, Number, and Case: both feminine gender, singular number; 'she'—nominative case, 'her'—objective case.

5. 'Them,' 'less,' 'thee.'—'Them,' third personal pronoun, inflected for Number and Case; plural number, objective case. 'Less,' adverb, ('little'), inflected for Degree; comparative degree. 'Thee,' second personal pronoun, inflected for Number and Case; singular number, objective case.

6. 'Those,' 'who,' 'me.'—'Those,' demonstrative pronoun 'that,' inflected for Number; plural number. 'Who,' relative pronoun, inflected for Case; nominative case. 'Who' is here plural, but has no inflection to express this: we must refer to the antecedent 'those,' or to the inflection of the

verb 'love,' before we know the number of 'who.' 'Me,' first personal pronoun, inflected for Number and Case; singular number, objective case.

7. 'He,' 'whose,' 'empires,' 'stakes,' 'thrones.'—'Whose,' relative pronoun, inflected for Case; possessive case. 'Empires,' 'stakes,' 'thrones,' nouns inflected for Number; plural number.

8. 'Whom,' 'gods.'—'Gods,' noun, inflected for Number; plural number.

9. 'I,' 'its,' 'fullest.'—'I,' first personal pronoun, inflected for Number and Case; singular number, nominative case. 'Fullest,' adjective, ('full,') inflected for Degree; superlative degree.

10. 'These,' 'affairs,' 'moment's.'—'These,' demonstrative pronominal adjective, 'this,' inflected for Number; plural number. [This is an opportunity for putting the question whether adjectives generally are inflected for Number.] 'Affairs,' noun inflected for Number; plural number. 'Moment's,' noun inflected for Case; possessive case.

11. 'I,' 'courts,' 'affairs,' 'debts,' 'prayers.'—The four nouns are inflected for the plural number. Two of them, 'courts' and 'debts,' ending in sharp mutes, form the plural in sharp *s*: the other two, 'affairs' and 'prayers,' ending in a liquid 'r,' form the plural with the *z* sound of 's.'

12. 'Amends,' 'those,' 'prince's,' 'coffers.'—'Amends' is one of those nouns that are used only in the plural: the 's' has its *z* sound. 'Prince's,' noun inflected for case; possessive case. 'Coffers,' noun inflected for Number; plural number :the 's' has its *z* sound.

13. 'These,' 'writings,' 'counterfeits,' 'contents.'—'Writings.' 'Writing' is an abstract noun, active verbal; abstract nouns are not used in the plural until they have laid aside their character and become general nouns. 'Writings' must be parsed as the plural of a general noun; the name not of an abstract process, but of an actual thing. 'Counterfeits,' is another case of a noun originally abstract treated as a general noun, and used in the plural. 'Contents,' is used only in the plural. In 'writings,' the 's' comes after a flat mute 'g,' and sounds *z*: in the other two, 's' sounds sharp.

14. 'We,' 'manners.'—'We,' first personal pronoun, inflected for Number and Case; plural number, nominative case. 'Manners,' is used in this sense only in the plural: the singular 'manner' has a different meaning.

15. 'His,' 'compasses,' 'God's,' 'things.'—'His,' demonstrative pronoun, inflected for Gender, Number, and Case; masculine gender, singular number, possessive case. 'Compasses,' plural inflection in 'es' after a sibilant: 'compass' is one of those nouns that have the plural and the singular of different meanings. 'God's,' noun inflected for Case; possessive case. [Here the pupils may be asked what nouns the possessive inflection is chiefly confined to.] 'Things,' noun inflected for number; plural number.

16. 'Animals,' 'wiser,' 'sons,' 'men,' 'particulars.'—'Animals,' plural in *z* sound, after a liquid. 'Wiser,' adjective 'wise,' inflected for Degree; comparative degree. 'Sons,' plural in *z* sound after a liquid. 'Men,' plural formed by the obsolete mode of changing the vowel of the singular. 'Particulars,' plural in *z* sound after a liquid.

'Their' is not the possessive case of 'they,' but the possessive adjective. In the word 'compass,' we see the different meaning of 'compasses' in the singular form.

17. 'Softer,' 'petals,' 'roses,' 'dews,' 'waters,' 'walls,' 'gentlier,' 'eyelids,' 'eyes.'—'Softer' is properly the comparative degree of the adjective 'soft,' but here it is used, by poetical licence, as the comparative degree of the adverb 'softly.' 'Petals,' plural in *z* sound, after a liquid. 'Roses,' plural in *z* sound. [In this or in some similar case, the teacher may remark that 's' has its *z* sound after a sibilant.] 'Dews,' plural in *z* sound, after a vowel sound. 'Waters,' plural in *z* sound, after a liquid. 'Walls,' plural in *z* sound, after a liquid. 'Gentlier,' adverb 'gently' inflected for Degree; comparative degree. 'Eyelids,' plural in *z* sound, after a flat mute. 'Eyes,' plural in *z* sound, after a vowel.

18. 'He,' 'best,' 'more,' 'worst,' 'better.'—'Best,' adjective 'good' irregularly inflected for Degree; superlative degree. 'More,' adjective 'much' irregularly inflected for Degree; comparative degree. 'Worst,' adjective 'bad' irregularly inflected for Degree; superlative degree. 'Better,' adjective 'good' irregularly inflected for Degree; comparative degree.

When an adjective turns up in the Comparative or the Superlative degree, the pupils may be called upon to give the full Comparison.

Inflection of Verbs.

Answers to Questions—(p. 153).

Q. 2. Difference of voice means difference of form in the verb according as the agent or the object of the action (the *patient)* is the subject of the verb. When the agent is the subject of the verb, as—'The porter opened the gates,' the verb is said to be in the Active voice: when the object of the action is the subject of the verb, as—'The gates were opened by the porter,' the verb is said to be in the Passive voice.

Intransitive verbs have no Passive voice, because they have no object.

To signify the Passive voice, we make use of what is called an auxiliary to the inflection for the Passive voice, the verb 'to be.'

The teacher may here, if he thinks fit, add that certain intransitive verbs, such as 'sleep,' 'die,' 'fall,' are sometimes called *Neuter* verbs, that is, verbs *neither* Active nor Passive. Such verbs, as contrasted with 'walk,' 'run,' 'sing,' 'see,' are really more nearly allied to the Passive voice than to the Active: the subject of such verbs is not so much an agent as a passive object. Some grammarians, accordingly, make a distinction among Intransitive verbs corresponding to the distinction between Active and Passive; and parse them as *Active* Intransitives and *Neuter* Intransitives.

Q. 3. Difference of Mood means difference of form in the verb to express difference of *mode* or manner in the action.

Q. 5-9. The agreements and differences of the various parts of speech in '*ing*' should be tabulated and written on the black board—an important exercise.

THE INFINITIVE IN 'ING'—

Agrees with THE VERBAL NOUN IN 'ING' in the following:—

1. It may be the subject or the object of a verb.
2. It may be qualified by an adjective, especially the definite article, or a possessive adjective.

Differs from the verbal noun in 'ing' in the following:—

1. It takes an object, when transitive.
2. It may be qualified by an adverb.
3. It is never conjoined with the indefinite article.
4. It cannot be inflected for number.

The points of distinction between the Infinitive and the Participle of the same form may be stated thus:—

THE INFINITIVE IN 'ING'—

Agrees with THE PARTICIPLE IN 'ING' in the following:—

1. It takes an object when transitive.
2. It may be qualified by an adverb.
3. It expresses an action or event, not a quality.

Differs from the Participle in 'ing' in the following:—

1. It may be the subject or the object of a verb.
2. It cannot be an adjunct of a noun.
3. It expresses no particular time.

If, finally, we contrast the Infinitive in 'ing' with the Adjective of the same form, we find the following results:—

THE INFINITIVE IN 'ING'—

Agrees with THE ADJECTIVE IN 'ING' in nothing except in being a Part of Speech.

Differs from the Adjective in 'ing' in the following:—

1. It may be the subject or the object of a verb.
2. It cannot qualify a noun.
3. It takes an object, when transitive.

There is no risk of confounding the Infinitive with the Adjective of the same form: so that the tabulation of their differences is rather a refinement of distinguishing than a matter of practical service. It is chiefly the Infinitive and the Verbal Noun that there is any danger of confounding. The following is a table of the agreements and differences between them, from the point of view of the Verbal Noun (Q. 7):—

THE VERBAL NOUN IN 'ING'—

Agrees with THE INFINITIVE IN 'ING' in the following:—

1. It may be the subject or the object of a verb.
2. It may be qualified by an adjective.

Differs from the Infinitive in 'ing' in the following:—

1. It may be inflected for Number.
2. It may have the indefinite article before it.
3. It cannot take an object after it.
4. It cannot be qualified by an adverb.

The chief distinction of the verbal noun from the infinitive, in the absence of Inflection, is the indefinite article: just as the chief distinction of the infinitive from the verbal noun is the taking an object or a qualifying adverb.

As an exercise in distinguishing parts of speech, the pupil may be asked to distinguish the verbal noun from the participle and from the adjective; though in actual parsing there is no risk of confounding them.

THE VERBAL NOUN IN 'ING'—

Agrees with THE PARTICIPLE IN 'ING' in no grammatical function.

Differs from the Participle in 'ing' in the following:—

1. It may be the subject or the object of a verb.
2. It may be inflected for number.
3. It cannot be an adjunct of a noun.
4. It expresses no particular time.
5. It cannot take an object or an adverb.

THE VERBAL NOUN IN 'ING'—

Agrees with THE ADJECTIVE IN 'ING' in no grammatical function.

Differs from the Adjective in 'ing' in the following:—

1. It may be the subject or the object of a verb.
2. It may be inflected for Number.
3. It cannot qualify a noun.

In the case of the Participle in 'ing' the chief difficulty arises in distinguishing it under certain circumstances from the Adjective of the same form (Q. 8). The agreements and differences of these two Parts of Speech may be tabulated as follows:—

THE PARTICIPLE IN 'ING'—

Agrees with THE ADJECTIVE IN 'ING' in the following:—

1. It may be an Adjunct of a noun.

Differs from the Adjective in 'ing' in the following:—

1. It expresses an action, not a quality.
2. It expresses a particular time.
3. It cannot be inflected for degree.

This distinction is the most important in connection with the Participle in 'ing,' as being the one most likely to be neglected. The agreements and differences of the Participle in 'ing' and the Infinitive and the Verbal Noun of the same form, have been already tabulated: the teacher, if he thinks it necessary to make the variation, will easily modify the tables so as to suit the point of view of the Participle.

The distinction between the Adjective and the Participle in 'ing' is of such importance that it may be repeated from the point of view of the Adjective.

THE ADJECTIVE IN 'ING'—

Agrees with THE PARTICIPLE IN 'ING' in the following:—

1. It is an adjunct of a noun.

Differs from the Participle in 'ing' in the following:—

1. It expresses a quality, not an action.
2. It may be inflected for degree.
3. It expresses no particular time.

Q. 10. The infinitive is called a Gerund, when it expresses a purpose. The infinitive in *ing*, preceded by the preposition 'for,' has the same meaning, and may receive the same name.

In stating the differences between the infinitive in *ing* and the participle of the same form, it was mentioned that the infinitive could not be used as an adjunct of a noun. This holds as regards the infinitive proper. But in its gerundial sense, by a process of ellipsis, the infinitive may be used as a sort of adjective phrase. In such expressions as—'scissors *to grind*,' 'a house *to let*,'—the gerunds 'to grind' and 'to let,' are virtually adjective phrases, qualifying the the nouns 'scissors' and 'house.'

Q. 14, 15. 'Trust' and 'shake' are verbs of the New and of the Old Conjugations respectively. The inflection for

Tense, Number, and Person, corresponds to the inflections of 'Call' and 'Drive' at p. 135 of the Grammar.

Q. 18. The black-board may be used to give prominence to the inflections made with auxiliaries. The teacher may write up such abbreviated tables as the following:—

INFLECTIONS WITH THE AUXILIARY 'TO BE.'

Passive Voice—'Be' joined to perfect participle, 'I am called.'

Progressive Tense—'Be' joined to imperfect participle, 'I am calling.'

INFLECTIONS WITH THE AUXILIARY 'TO HAVE.'

Present Perfect Tense—Present of 'Have' joined with perf. part., 'I *have* called.'

Past Perfect Tense—Past of 'Have' joined with perf. part., 'I *had* called.'

Perfect Participle Active—Imperf. part. of 'Have' joined with perf. part., '*having* called.'

Continuous Tenses—'Have,' 'had,' &c., joined with 'been' and impf. part., 'I *have* been calling,' 'I *had* been calling.'

Q. 22. The various uses of 'Do' may be numbered and tabulated to assist the memory.

'DO' IS USED IN VARIOUS FORMS OF THE VERB.

1. In the *Emphatic* form—I *do* believe you.
2. In the *Interrogative* form—*Do* you believe me?
3. In the *Negative* form—You *do* not believe me.
4. As a *Substitute* for another verb—Do you believe me? I *do*.

Q. 23. The various meanings of 'May' may be similarly tabulated.

'MAY' EXPRESSES:—

1. *Permission*—You *may* go.
2. *Possibility*, or *Concession*—It *may* be true.
3. *A Wish*—*May* you be happy.

Q. 24. The various uses of 'Must' are numbered in the Grammar, and can hardly be further abbreviated.

Exercise 16—(p. 133).

Infinitive, Participle, Adjective, Verbal Noun, and *Gerund.*

1. 'To live,' infinitive. The infinitive phrase 'to live in suspense,' is here used in place of a noun, in apposition to 'it,' the grammatical subject of the sentence. 'In suspense,' is an adjective phrase, completion of the incomplete verb 'live.'

2. 'Talking,' infinitive in 'ing.' 'Talking,' in this connection, will stand both the tests that distinguish the Infinitive from the Verbal Noun: it has an object—'overmuch'—after it, and it could not in this meaning have the indefinite article 'a' before it. We know that it is not a participle from its being the subject of the sentence. By way of exercise, one may put the questions—How do you know that it is not a verbal noun in *ing*; and—How do you know that it is not a participle in *ing*?

3. 'To learn,' and 'to hear' are both infinitives. 'To learn' stands in place of a noun in apposition to 'it:' and 'to hear' stands in place of a noun as the object of the verb 'learn.'

The pupil should be asked how he knows that these infinitives are not Gerunds; and should answer—Because they do not express any purpose.

4. 'Trembling,' is here a Verbal Noun. We know that it is not a participle from its being the subject of the sentence; and we know that it is not an infinitive from its taking the indefinite article 'a' before it.

5. 'Pushing,' imperfect participle in 'ing.' How do we know that it is not an infinitive? Because it does not stand in any of the places occupied by Nouns, but qualifies the subject of the sentence in the manner of a co-ordinate Adjective. How do we know that 'pushing' is not a participial Adjective? It has no object after it; is it distinguished from the Adjective in any other way? The only obvious and palpable distinction is that it expresses an action going on at a particular time.

'Realised,' perfect Participle, distinguished from the adjective by its expressing an action completed at a particular time.

6. 'Piercing,' an Adjective, restrictive, expressing a quality or property of the cry. The quality of the cry is expressed without regard to time.

'Startled,' on the other hand, is a perfect Participle. Being startled is not a property or quality of the air, but an effect completed at that particular time.

7. 'Stricken,' though it has the form of a perfect Participle, is here a restrictive Adjective. It is used to constitute a smaller class 'stricken deer,' that is 'wounded deer,' within the larger class 'deer.' In such a sentence as—'Stricken with a fatal wound, the poor deer sought the covert to die;' 'stricken' is a participle, expressing an action as completed

at a particular time, after which something else happened. Had the meaning here been, 'Let the deer having been stricken—when it has been stricken—go weep,' 'stricken' must have been parsed as a perfect Participle on the ground that it expressed time. But the meaning is—'the deer that has been stricken,' no matter when: and accordingly 'stricken' must be taken as an Adjective.

'Ungalled,' is an Adjective without any doubt, there being no verb 'ungall.'

'Go weep,' equivalent to—go *to* weep, go *for the purpose of* weeping. 'Weep' must here probably be parsed as the Gerund use of the infinitive, with the sign of the infinitive omitted.

8. 'Loathing,' 'dreading,' are Participles, expressing actions going on at the time of the principal verb 'live.' Both of them have objects after them, and so cannot be mistaken for adjectives.

'To die,' an Infinitive, object after 'dreading.' How do we know that it is not a Gerund? Because it does not express any purpose.

9. 'Doing,' Infinitive in 'ing.' It is neither an Adjective nor a Participle, for it is the subject of a sentence: and it is readily distinguished from the verbal noun of the same form by its having an object after it.

'Disinterested,' is an Adjective: there is no verb 'disinterest.'

10. 'To please,' seeing that it expresses purpose, being equivalent to 'that I might please,' must be regarded as the Gerund use of the infinitive.

'To enforce,' 'to enchant,' are also Gerunds, expressing purpose—'spirits for the purpose of enforcing,' 'arts for the purpose of enchanting.'

'Ending,' must here probably be parsed as a verbal Noun, though there is really nothing to distinguish it from the infinitive in *ing*. The Infinitive, as well as the Noun, may take a possessive Adjective, and may stand as the subject of a sentence.

11. 'To tell,' Gerund, equivalent to 'for the purpose of telling,' or 'that I may tell.'

Exercise 17.

Verb Inflections generally.

1. 'Translating,' and 'drawing after the life,' are probably Infinitives in *ing*, but the form of the text gives us no decisive means of concluding whether they are Infinitives or verbal Nouns. In the case of 'translating' we have simply a bare word in *ing* standing as the subject of a sentence: it has no object to fix it as an infinitive, and no indefinite article to fix it as a Noun. In the other case, 'drawing after the life,' the adverbial phrase 'after the life' would seem to fix 'drawing' as a Verb and not as a Noun. It might indeed be argued that 'after the life' is an adjective phrase qualifying the Noun 'drawing:' but this rather does violence to the meaning. If the sentence had been—'A translation is a kind of drawing after the life,' 'drawing' would then have been a verbal Noun qualified by an adjective phrase: but as it is, when we consider the meaning, we must pronounce both 'translating' and 'drawing' infinitives in *ing*.

2. 'Weeping,' probably an Infinitive in *ing*.

'May.' In handling this exercise, the teacher should first ask —In which of its meanings is 'may' used here? *Ans.* In its meaning of *possibility* or *concession*, the meaning of the clause being—'It is *possible* that weeping endure for a night,' or, 'I admit that weeping may endure for a night.' Having received this answer, or given this explanation, the teacher should next ask—What is 'may' inflected for? The strict answer to this is—For *Tense* alone. If we look to the word 'may' alone and not to the subject, we see only that 'may' is in the Present tense: we do not know whether it is in the First Person or in the Third Person, in the Singular Number or in the Plural Number. When we look to the subject, we see that 'may' is in the Third Person and in the Singular Number; but we do not see this by looking to 'may' alone; by so doing we can know only the Tense. We may be said to know also the Voice: but no reference should be made to Voice except in verbs that have two Voices.

Such cross-examination as this is necessary now and then to awaken the mind to the exact nature of Inflection. For ordinary purposes the pupil may be expected to parse in some such form as this:—'May,' a verb of incomplete predication, having the infinitive '(to) endure' as its complement; used here in its meaning of *Possibility* or *Concession*; third person singular, Present Indicative. This is full parsing for Parts of Speech as well as for Inflection: if only parsing for Inflection is required, 'third person singular, Present Indicative' would be enough.

Another way of parsing 'may,' as a Part of Speech, is to regard it as a Transitive verb, having the infinitive '(to) endure' as its object.

'Endure,' indefinite infinitive of intransitive verb, with the sign 'to' omitted; parsed as the complement or the object of 'may' according as we consider 'may' a verb of incomplete predication, or a transitive verb.

'Cometh'—*Part of Speech :* –intransitive verb. *Inflection :* —third person singular, present indicative indefinite. 'Cometh' is inflected for Person, Number, Tense, and Mood: we know all these particulars by looking to 'cometh' alone, without regard to its subject. The verb being intransitive, we do not refer to the Voice.

The case of 'cometh' may be made an opportunity for remarking on the meaning of the Present Indefinite, as the tense that expresses what is true *at all times.*

3. 'Shall.'—*Part of Speech :*—verb of incomplete predication, having for its complement the infinitive '(to) fade.' 'Shall' is not here the auxiliary of the inflection for Future Time: the third person singular of the Future Tense of 'fade' is '*will* fade.' 'Shall fade' has the meaning of futurity and something more: it has the peculiar meaning of the incomplete verb 'shall,' namely, obligation, necessity. The meaning of the sentence is—'It cannot but be that thy eternal summer will not fade.' *Inflection :*—Looking to 'shall' alone we know only that it is in the Present Tense; we do not know whether it is in the First Person or in the Third Person, in the Singular or in the Plural, in the Indicative Mood or in the Subjunctive. But looking also to the subject and to the form of the sentence, we see that it is in the—third person singular, present indicative.

'Fade.'—*Part of Speech :*—Intransitive verb. *Inflection :*—infinitive, complement of the incomplete verb 'shall.'

'Shall' like 'may,' may be regarded as a transitive verb, having the infinitive '(to) fade' as its object.

4. 'See.'—*Part of Speech :*—transitive verb, object 'matter.' *Inflection :*—From all that we know by looking

only to the word 'see,' it might be the first person singular, present indicative, or any person in the plural of that tense. But when we look to the rest of the sentence, we find that 'see' is here the Imperative form of the verb.

Being in the passive voice, it has no object: the object of the action that it expresses is here its grammatical subject.

'Endued.'—*Part of Speech*:—transitive verb. *Inflection*:—Perfect participle, passive voice. The pupil may here be reminded that the perfect participle of transitive verbs is always passive.

'Press.' *Part of Speech*:—intransitive verb. 'Press' is usually a transitive verb; but like the allied verb 'push,' it has passed into an intransitive meaning. *Inflection*:—infinitive indefinite. This infinitive must be taken as the secondary or indirect object of 'see:' but in point of fact, the infinitive here is a poetical license. Strict grammar would require the participle 'pressing,' the whole of the second line being a participial adjunct of the object 'matter.'

Another way of parsing 'press' would be to regard 'see' as a verb of incomplete predication, and 'press' as an infinitive complement with the sign of the infinitive omitted as is the case after 'may,' 'can,' and other incomplete verbs 'See' would then be a transitive verb as regarded 'matter,' and an incomplete verb as regarded 'press.'

5. 'Was predisposed.' *Part of Speech*:—transitive verb. *Inflection*:—passive voice, third person singular, past indicative indefinite. We may know voice, person, number, tense, and mood, by looking simply to the verb. To keep beginners awake to the mechanism of inflection, the teacher should ask—what part of speech 'was' is, what 'predisposed' is by itself, how the past tense is made up, and what inflec-

tions the verb 'predispose' undergoes without the aid of auxiliaries. Such questions may be repeated now and then when a passive turns up.

'To think.' *Part of Speech* :—transitive verb, having 'ill' as an object. *Inflection* :—infinitive indefinite. The infinitive is here really an object after the preposition 'to,' the meaning being that 'he was predisposed to *thinking* ill, &c.' In strict grammar the full expression would be 'predisposed *to* to think ill.' We must suppose that 'to' the preposition, and 'to' the sign of the infinitive, have been confusedly run into one.

'Requiring.' *Part of Speech* :—transitive verb, object—'words.' *Inflection* :—participle impcrfect. We know that it is not an infinitive from its being an adjectival adjunct of 'causes:' and that it is not an adjective, from its having an object.

6. 'Maketh.' *Part of Speech* :—transitive verb, object—'father.' *Inflection* :—Active voice, third person singular, present indicative indefinite. See 'cometh,' No. 2.

7. 'Examine.' Refer back to 'see,' No. 4. *Part of Speech* :—transitive verb, object—the clauses after 'whether,' to end of sentence. These clauses are called Noun Clauses, because they stand in place of nouns. *Inflection* :—Active voice, imperative mood.

'Be.' *Part of Speech* :—verb of incomplete predication, complement—'true.' *Inflection* :—third person singular, present subjunctive. There is nothing in the form of the word itself to indicate of what person or of what number it is: to know this we must look to the subject.

8. 'Have.' *Part of Speech* :—transitive verb. *Inflection* :

—active voice, second person plural, present indicative. Before we can be sure of person, number, or mood, we must look to the context.

'To conceive.' *Part of Speech* :—transitive verb, here used intransitively, no object being directly stated. *Inflection* :—infinitive, gerund meaning.

'To deter,' and 'to execute,' are parsed exactly like 'to conceive.'

9. 'Tell.' *Part of Speech* :—transitive verb, object—'can this be death' (Noun Clause). *Inflection* :—imperative mood.

'Can.' See Nos. 2 and 3, 'may' and 'shall.' *Part of Speech* :—verb of incomplete predication, quasi-auxiliary; complement—'be death.' *Inflection* :—third person singular, present indicative, interrogative form. We cannot tell person, number, or mood from looking merely to the inflection. The interrogative form consists here in placing the verb before the subject.

'Be,' infinitive with 'to' omitted, part of the complement of 'can.'

10. 'Did.' *Part of Speech* :—here a quasi-auxiliary verb, used in making up an Emphatic form. *Inflection* :—third person singular, past indicative.

'Lie.' *Part of Speech* :—transitive verb, object—'tempest.' *Inflection* :—infinitive indefinite : used after 'did' to make up the emphatic form of the first person singular past indefinite indicative, of the active voice of the verb 'to see.'

'Dropping.' *Part of Speech* :—transitive verb 'fire.' *Inflection* :—active voice, imperfect participle. We know that it is not an infinitive from its being an adjectival adjunct of 'tempest;' and that it is not an adjective from its having an object.

11. 'Shall.' *Part of Speech:*—see No. 3. If it is taken as an incomplete verb, the complement is 'be an abhorring.' 'Be,' itself an incomplete verb, cannot alone complete a predicate. *Inflection:*—third person plural, present indicative. 'Shall' is not distinctively inflected for either person or number, except in the second person singular.

'Abhorring' is here a verbal noun. The indefinite article is decisive.

12. One way of parsing 'be' is to suppose an ellipsis of 'may' in its function of expressing a wish, and to regard 'be' as an infinitive after 'may,' and part of its complement.

Otherwise, we must suppose this to be a peculiar use of the third person singular, present subjunctive, for the purpose of expressing a wish.

'Skirts.' *Part of Speech:*—transitive verb, object—'down.' *Inflection:*—active voice, third person singular, present indicative indefinite. The inflection in this case is distinctive for person, number, and mood: no other person either of the singular or of the plural has the same inflection.

13. 'Is.' *Part of Speech:*—here the auxiliary of the Passive inflection. *Inflection:*—third person singular, present indicative.

'Apprehended.' *Part of Speech:*—transitive verb. *Inflection:*—passive voice, perfect participle: used along with the auxiliary 'is' to make up the third person singular present indefinite indicative of the passive voice of the verb 'to apprehend.'

'Has.' *Part of Speech*:—here an auxiliary verb, used with 'been' to make up the present perfect of the passive voice. *Inflection*:—third person singular, present indicative.

'Been.' Auxiliary of the passive voice; perfect participle.

'Overcome.' *Part of Speech*:—transitive verb. *Inflection*:—passive voice, perfect participle, used with the auxiliaries 'has' and 'been' to make up the third person singular present perfect indicative of the passive voice of the verb 'to overcome.'

14. 'Would.' *Part of Speech*:—not an auxiliary verb here, but a verb of incomplete predication without any reference to Future time. It is completed by the infinitive '(to) play.' *Inflection*:—third person plural, past indicative.

'Play.' *Part of speech*:—intransitive verb. *Inflection*:—infinitive indefinite, with 'to' omitted, complement of 'would.' 'Would play' does not express future time from a past point, but means 'were willing (or were pleased) to play.'

15. 'Rushed.' *Part of Speech*:—intransitive verb. *Inflection*:—third person plural, past indefinite indicative of the verb 'to rush.'

'Driven.' *Part of Speech*:—transitive verb. *Inflection*:—passive voice, perfect participle.

16. 'Leave.' *Part of Speech*:—transitive verb, object—'me.' *Inflection*:—active voice, imperative mood (used in the sense of entreaty).

'Diest.' *Part of Speech*:—intransitive verb (neuter) *Inflection*:—second person singular, present indefinite indicative. The second person singular is very rarely used, the plural form being used along with 'you,' which is the ordinary pronoun of the second person (Gram., p. 44).

'Know.' *Part of Speech* :—transitive verb, object—'where to go.' *Inflection* :—active voice, first person singular present indefinite indicative.

'To go.' *Part of Speech* :—intransitive verb. *Inflection* :—infinitive gerund. 'Where to go' is equivalent to 'any place that I may go to,' or 'any place useful *for going* to.' The phrase is elliptical: the gerund must be parsed as an adverbial qualification.

17. 'Tolls.' *Part of Speech* :—transitive verb, object—'knell.' *Inflection* :—active voice, third person singular, present indefinite indicative.

'Parting.' *Part of Speech* :—intransitive verb. *Inflection* :—imperfect participle. 'Parting' is not here an adjective: it does not express a quality of 'day,' but an action that the day is supposed to be undergoing at the time of the tolling of the curfew.

'Lowing,' is also the imperfect participle of an intransitive verb. 'The lowing herd' are not a separate class of animals from the herd that do not low: the word 'lowing' expresses an action of the herd at a particular time, and so is a participle and not an adjective.

'Winds.' *Part of Speech* :—intransitive verb. *Inflection* :—third person singular, present indefinite indicative.

18. 'Wouldst.' *Part of Speech* :—the auxiliary of the Future tense, used here by a peculiar idiom to express contingent futurity, future action in a supposed case. 'Wouldst thou demolish a driven leaf'—*if it came in thy way*, or with some such supposition. *Inflection* :—second person singular, past indicative.

'Demolish.' *Part of Speech* :—transitive verb, object—

'leaf.' *Inflection* :—infinitive indefinite, used with the auxiliary 'wouldst' to make up a tense of contingent futurity for the verb 'to demolish.'

'Driven.' *Part of Speech* :—transitive verb. *Inflection* :—passive voice, perfect participle; a participle under circumstances where the word *might be* an adjective.

19. 'Hast.' *Part of Speech* :—auxiliary verb, used with 'forgotten' to make up the present perfect tense. *Inflection* :—second person singular, present indicative. Here as in Nos. 9 and 18, the interrogative form consists in putting the auxiliary or quasi-auxiliary verb before the subject.

'Forgotten.' *Part of Speech* :—transitive verb, object—'how soon we must sever' (Noun Clause). *Inflection* :—active voice, perfect participle, used with 'past' to make up the present perfect indicative of the verb 'to forget.'

'Must.' *Part of Speech* :—quasi-auxiliary verb, here used in its meaning of 'compulsion from without.' *Inflection* :—'Must' is invariable for tense, number, and person; but we know by looking to the context that it is here in the first person plural past indicative.

'Sever.' *Part of Speech* :—intransitive verb. *Inflection* :—infinitive indefinite, completion of the incomplete verb 'must.'

20. 'Gave.' *Part of Speech* :—transitive verb, object—'way.' 'Gave way' is so common a combination, and is used in a sense so far independent of the literal meaning of the words 'give' and 'way,' that it may be taken as a compound verb. *Inflection* :—active voice, third person singular, past indefinite indicative.

'Consented.' *Part of Speech* :—intransitive verb. 'Consented to,' may also be taken as a compound verb. *Inflection* :—third person singular, past indefinite indicative.

'Ruined,' transitive verb, active voice, third person singular, past indefinite indicative.

'Pending.' *Part of Speech* :—intransitive verb. *Inflection* :—imperfect participle.

'Generated.' Parsed like 'ruined.'

'Leading.' *Part of Speech* :—transitive verb. *Inflection* :—active voice, imperfect participle. 'Leading' is obviously a co-ordinate participle. 'Pending' might at first glance be taken as restrictive, but when we look narrowly we see that 'the negotiations' would alone be sufficient to denote the negotiations referred to, and that 'pending' superadds information about them, and so is co-ordinate.

21. 'Should.' *Part of Speech* :—Auxiliary verb, used to express a supposed future time. *Inflection* :—second person plural past indicative of the verb 'shall.'

'See.' *Part of Speech* :—transitive verb, object—'flock.' *Inflection* :—infinitive indefinite, used along with the auxiliary 'should' to make up a tense of supposed futurity for the verb 'see.'

'Picking.' *Part of Speech* :—transitive verb, objects—'where (it liked),' and 'what it liked.' *Inflection* :—active voice, imperfect participle.

'Liked.' *Part of Speech* :—transitive verb, object—'what.' *Inflection* :—third person singular, past indefinite indicative.

'Taking.' Parsed like 'picking.'

'Wanted,' Parsed like 'liked.' In order to bring out what is the object of 'wanted,' we must state the full expression for the elliptical clause 'as much as it wanted:' which is—'as much as *the quantity that* it wanted.' 'That,' understood, is the object of 'wanted.'

'Gathering,' 'reserving,' 'keeping.' Parsed like 'picking.'

'Got.' *Part of Speech*:—transitive verb, object—'that' understood. *Inflection*:—third person plural, past indefinite indicative.

'Sitting.' *Part of Speech*:—intransitive verb. *Inflection*:—imperfect participle.

'Looking.' Parsed like 'sitting.' 'Looking on,' is a compound verb.

'Was.' *Part of Speech*:—auxiliary verb, used in making up the Past Progressive tense. *Inflection*:—third person singular, past indicative.

'Devouring.' *Part of Speech*:—transitive verb, object—'it.' *Inflection*:—imperfect participle, used with 'was' to make up the Past Progressive tense of the verb 'to devour.'

'Throwing,' and 'wasting,' are parsed like 'devouring.' 'Was' is understood to each of them. 'Throwing about' is a compound verb.

'Touched.' *Part of Speech*:—transitive verb. *Inflection*:—third person singular, past indefinite subjunctive. We do not know that the mood is subjunctive until we look to the conjunction of Condition, 'if.'

'Flying' and 'tearing' are participles. 'Flying' itself is an intransitive verb: but if we take 'flying upon' as a compound verb, we may regard the compound as transitive, having 'it' as an object.

'Would.' *Part of Speech*:—here, as in No. 8, an auxiliary verb used to express contingent futurity. *Inflection*:—second person plural, past indicative of 'will.'

'Practised.' *Part of Speech*:—transitive verb. *Inflection*:—passive voice, perfect participle: used along with 'is' to make up the third person singular, present indefinite indicative passive of the verb 'to practise.'

'Established.' Parsed like 'practised.'

22. 'Mouldering,' 'drenching,' 'driving.' These words are very much of the nature of adjectives. They point rather to inseparable qualities than to passing actions. It could hardly be considered an error to parse them as imperfect participles of intransitive verbs: but it is probably more correct to take them as adjectives. They are all co-ordinate adjectives: they cannot be said to restrict.

'Beat.' *Part of Speech*:—intransitive verb: but if it is taken along with 'on' as a compound verb, the compound is transitive, governing 'bones' as object. *Inflection*:—perfect participle: used with the auxiliary 'have' to form the third person plural present perfect indicative active of the verb 'to beat.'

Let.' *Part of Speech*:—transitive verb, object—'(to) sleep.' *Inflection*:—active voice, imperative mood.

'Sleep.' *Part of Speech*:—intransitive verb (neuter). *Inflection*:—infinitive indefinite, with sign 'to' omitted, used as object of the verb 'let.'

SYNTAX.

ANALYSIS OF SENTENCES.

Answers to Questions—(p. 175).

The only question in this series that cannot be answered by a repetition or simple modification of the words of the Grammar is No. 15. In such a sentence as—'He that hath ears to hear, let him hear,' the relative clause, 'that hath ears to hear,' must not be regarded as directly qualifying the pronoun. A pronoun cannot be either enlarged or restricted by an adjective, because, indeed, being merely a word of reference, it has no independent meaning to enlarge, restrict, or qualify in any way. A relative clause coming after a personal pronoun serves the purpose of declaring the reference of the pronoun: to explain its position thoroughly, we must suppose the omission of a noun in apposition, which noun, and not the pronoun, is restricted or enlarged by the relative clause. We must suppose the full expression to be—'He, *I mean, the man* that hath ears to hear, let him hear.' So in the sentence—'Them that honour me, I will honour,' we may suppose the full expression to be—'Them, *I mean the persons* that honour me, &c.' See **Exercise** 18, Nos. 16, 33.

All adjuncts of Pronouns must be of the nature of nouns in apposition, making known the actual reference. Thus, in the sentence (Grammar, p. 42)—'I, James Brown, of Duke

Street, St. James's, do hereby declare'—'James Brown, of Duke Street, St. James's,' must be analysed as a noun with adjuncts in apposition to the pronoun 'I.' Similarly, in the sentence—'We English occupy a middle ground &c.,' 'English' is a noun in apposition to 'we.'

For other instances turn to Exercise 7, No. 20 (p. 54); Exercise 15, No. 7 (p. 129); Exercise 17, No. 9 (p. 151).

'It is my wish that you, my boy, should visit the places &c.' 'My boy' is analysed as a noun with a possessive adjective, in apposition to 'you.'

'Yes! where is he, the champion and the child,
Of all that's great or little, wise or wild;
Whose game was empires, and whose stakes were thrones.'

All this sentence after 'he,' describes what 'he' refers to, and is analysed as being in apposition to 'he.' 'Is' has here its meaning of 'exists;' 'where' is an adverbial adjunct of the predicate; and 'he' is the subject. In a tabulated analysis of the sentence, the last part would appear as follows:—

II. *Nouns with Adjuncts in apposition to Subject*	1. 'the champion of all that's great or little, wise or wild.' 2. 'the child of all that's great or &c.' 3. 'whose game was empires.' 4. 'whose stakes were thrones.'

Take the other sentence indicated—'Tell me, my soul, can this be death.' Here the subject is 'thou' understood, and 'my soul' is in apposition to 'thou.'

There is room for a great deal of minute discussion regarding the exact force of a relative clause attached to a pronoun.

I believe the explanation of it by a supposed ellipsis to be the most satisfactory. It may be maintained that the relative clause is used to restrict the *reference* of the pronoun: but to this it may be objected that the function of the pronoun is to refer to something otherwise specified and made definite in the mind of the reader or hearer.

While a pronoun cannot be restricted, having no definite sphere to restrict, it may have a co-ordinate statement attached to it, either by a co-ordinating participle or by a co-ordinating relative. It cannot have a restrictive phrase or clause attached because it is supposed to refer to something already specified: but once having directed us to a specific something, it may have attached to it a co-ordinate phrase or clause superadding information about that something. Take for example the following sentence regarding princes:—'They, *being men and not gods*, can give wealth and titles, but not virtues.' Here the reference of 'they' is to a definite subject previously mentioned, and the participial phrase is a co-ordinate statement by way of explanation of the predicate. Take, as another example, the following, regarding an individual previously mentioned:—'He, who never murmured at his own misfortunes, now wept over the misfortunes of his friend.' Such phrases and clauses are quite common. They must be analysed as co-ordinate adjective clauses to the subject referred to by the pronoun. Other examples are:—'Hoping to see you soon, I am your affectionate friend;' 'Entering the house as a stranger, he at once made himself at home;' 'Overjoyed at their success, they now expected to carry everything before them.'

In handling the Analysis of Sentences, it may be found convenient to put on the black-board a table of the possible varieties of simple Subject, and the adjuncts admissible for each. Some such table as the following may answer the purpose:—

I. SUBJECT.	II. ATTRIBUTIVE ADJUNCTS OF SUBJECT.
NOUN	1. ADJECTIVE. 2. Noun for Adj. 3. Adverb for Adj. 4. Possessive case. 5. Noun in apposition. 6. Prepositional Phrase. 7. Participial Phrase. 8. Adjective clause.
Pronoun	Noun in apposition (with or without adjuncts). Co-ordinate participial phrase or relative clause.
Infinitive simple or with 1. Complement. 2. Object. 3. Adverb or Adverbial Phrase.	1. Definite article. 2. Possessive adjective. 3. Possessive case.

The same table will answer for the Object and its Attributive Adjuncts, the enlargements of the Object being the same as the enlargement of the Subject. For the Predicate we may draw up some such table as the following:—

III. SIMPLE PREDICATE.	VI. ADVERBIAL ADJUNCTS OF PREDICATE.
VERB: Simple, Compound, or Complex	1. ADVERB. 2. Adverbial Phrase in form of— (1) Noun. (2) Noun and Adjunct. (3) Preposition with noun. (4) Participle or Particip. Phrase. (5) Gerund or Infinitive. 3. Adverbial Clause.

These tables may be put on the black board side by side along with the Object and its Adjuncts, giving a sort of bird's eye view of the whole Analysis of Sentences.

Exercise 18—(p. 173).

Analysis of Sentences.

1. Amid the roses fierce Repentance rears
Her snaky crest.

I. *Subject,* 'Repentance.'

II. *Attributive adjunct of Subject* { 'fierce,' *adjective, co-ordinate.*

III. *Predicate,* 'rears.'

IV. *Object,* 'crest.'

V. *Attributive adjuncts of Object* { 'her,' *possessive adj.* 'snaky,' *adj. co-ordinate.*

VI. *Adverbial adjunct of Predicate* { 'amid the roses,' *adverbial phrase of Place.*

2. Man, the subject of Politics, can speak.

I. *Subject*, 'man.'

II. *Attributive Adjuncts of Subject* — 'the subject of Politics,' *noun, with adjuncts, in apposition.*

III. *Predicate*
- 1. *Verb of incomplete predication*, 'can.'
- 2. *Complement*, 'speak.'

3. Home they brought her warrior dead.

I. *Subject*, 'they.'

III. *Predicate*, 'brought.'

IV. *Object*, 'warrior.'

V. *Attributive Adjuncts of Object*
- 1. 'her,' *possessive adjective.*
- 2. 'dead,' *adjective, co-ordinate.*

VI. *Adverbial Adjuncts of Predicate* — 'home,' *adv. phrase of place, prep. omitted.*

4. His purpose is to avert bad consequences.

I. *Subject*,' 'purpose.'

II. *Attributive adjunct of Subject* — 'his,' *possessive adjective, restrictive.*

III. *Predicate*
- 1. *Verb of incomplete predication* 'is.'
- 2. *Complement*, 'to avert bad consequences,' *infinitive with object.*

5. It fell upon a raw and gusty day
The troubled Tiber chafing with his shores.

I. *Subject*, 'it.'

III. *Predicate*, 'fell.'

VI. *Adverbial adjuncts of Predicate*	1. 'upon a raw and gusty day.' *adv. phrase of time and circumstance.* 2. 'the troubled Tiber chafing with his shores,' *participial adverbial phrase of circumstance (Nominative Absolute).*

6. Now leave complaining, and begin your tea.

Compound Sentence.—A + B. [A] Now leave complaining; [B] begin your tea. A and B are united by the cumulative conjunction 'and.'

Analysis of A.

[I. *Subject*, 'you,' *understood.*]
III. *Predicate*, 'leave.'
IV. *Object*, 'complaining,' *infinitive.*
VI. *Adverbial adjunct of Predicate* } 'now,' *adverb of Time.*

Analysis of B.

[I. *Subject*, 'you,' *understood.*]
III. *Predicate*, 'begin.'
IV. *Object*, 'tea.'
VI. *Attributive Adjunct of Object* } 'your,' *possessive adjective.*

7. He loved planting and building, and brought in a politer way of living.

Compound Contracted Sentence.—A + B + C. [A] He loved planting; [B] (he loved) building; [C] (he) brought in a politer way of living. A, B, and C, are united by the cumulative conjunction 'and.'

ANALYSIS OF A.

I. *Subject*, 'he.'
III. *Predicate*, 'loved.'
IV. *Object*, 'planting,' *infinitive.*

ANALYSIS OF B.

I. *Subject*, 'he.'
III. *Predicate*, 'loved.'
IV. *Object*, 'building,' *infinitive.*

ANALYSIS OF C.

I. *Subject*, 'he.'
III. *Predicate*, 'brought in,' *compound verb.*
IV. *Object*, 'way.'
V. *Attributive Adjuncts of Object*
1. 'a,' *indefinite article.*
2. 'politer,' *adjective, comparative degree.*
3. 'of living,' *prepositional adj. phrase.*

8. Leaves have their time to fall,
And flowers to wither at the North Wind's breath.

COMPOUND CONTRACTED SENTENCE.—A + B. [A] Leaves have their time to fall; [B] flowers (have their time) to wither at the North Wind's breath. A and B are united by the cumulative conjunction 'and.'

ANALYSIS OF A.

I. *Subject*, 'leaves.'
III. *Predicate*, 'have.'
IV. *Object*, 'time.'

V. *Attributive Adjuncts of Object* { 1. 'their,' *possessive adj.* 2. 'to fall,' *gerundial adjective phrase.*

ANALYSIS OF B.

I. *Subject*, 'flowers.'

III. *Predicate*, 'have.'

IV. *Object*, 'time.'

V. *Attributive Adjuncts of Object* { 1. 'their,' *Possessive Adjunct.* 2. 'to wither at the North Wind's breath,' *gerundial adjective phrase.*

Note.—In this sentence the gerunds undoubtedly qualify the object, not the predicate verb, and so stand in place of adjectives. We may suppose the ellipsis of some such clause as 'that is set apart for.' In B the gerundial infinitive is qualified by an adverbial phrase of cause.

9. It was a shame for them to mar their complexions with long lying abed.

I. *Subject*, 'it.'

II. *Noun phrase in apposition to Subject* { 'to mar their complexions with long lying a-bed,' *infinitive, with object and adverbial adjuncts.*

III. *Predicate* { 1. *Verb of incomplete predication*, 'was.' 2. *Complement*, 'a shame.'

VI. *Adverbial Adjunct of Predicate* { 'for them,' *adverbial phrase of place.*

10. Now, therefore, let thy servant abide in place of the lad, a bondman to my lord.

[I. *Subject*, 'you,' *understood.*]

III. *Predicate*
1. *Verb of incomplete predication*, 'let.'
2. *Complement*, 'abide in place of the lad, a bondman,' &c., *infinitive, with two adverbial phrases of Manner.*

IV. *Object*, 'servant.'

V. *Attributive adjunct of Object* — 'They,' *possessive adjective.*

VI. *Adverbial Adjuncts of Predicate*
1. 'now,' *adverb of Time.*
2. 'therefore,' *adverb of Cause.*

Note.—'A bondman to my lord.' This must be taken as an adverbial qualification of 'abide.' We may suppose an ellipsis of 'for' or 'as.'

11. With droll sobriety they raised a smile
At Folly's cost, themselves unmoved the while.

I. *Subject*, 'they.'

III. *Predicate*, 'raised.'

IV. *Object*, 'smile.'

V. *Attributive adjunct of Object*, 'a.'

VI. *Attributive adjuncts of Predicate*
1. 'With droll sobriety,' *adv. phrase of Manner.*
2. 'At Folly's cost,' *adv. phrase of Cause.*
3. 'themselves unmoved the while,' *participial adverbial phrase of Manner (Nominative Absolute).*

12. Collecting, classifying, contrasting, and weighing facts, are processes made use of in teaching method.

I. *Subject*	'collecting, classifying, contrasting and weighing facts,' *a plural subject, made up by the cumulation of four infinitives, each with 'facts' as an object.*
III. *Predicate*	1. *Verb of incomplete predication,* 'are.' 2. *Complement,* 'processes made use of in teaching method,' *noun with compound adjunct.*

13. The boy stood on the burning deck,
Whence all but him had fled.

COMPLEX SENTENCE.—A + *a*.

I. *Subject,* 'boy.'
II. *Attributive adjunct of Subject,* 'the.'
III. *Predicate,* 'stood.'

VI. *Adverbial Adjuncts of Predicate*	'on the burning deck, whence all but him had fled,' *adverbial phrase of Place,* the noun 'deck' being enlarged by a *co-ordinate adjective phrase* —'whence all,' &c. (*a*).

ANALYSIS OF (*a*).

[I. *Subject,* 'men,' *understood.*]

II. *Attributive Adjunct of Subject*	'all but him,' *adjective qualified by adverbial phrase.*

III. *Predicate,* 'had fled.

VI. *Adverbial Adjunct of Predicate* { 'whence,' *pronominal adverb of place.*

14. The rose that all are praising, is not the rose for me.

' COMPLEX SENTENCE.—A + *a.*

I. *Subject,* 'rose.'

II. *Attributive Adjuncts of Subject* {
1. 'the.'
2. 'that all are praising,' *adjective clause* (*a*).

III. *Predicate* {
1. *Verb of incomplete predication,* 'is not.'
2. *Complement,* 'the rose for me,' *noun with adjuncts.*

ANALYSIS OF (*a*).

I. [*Subject,* 'persons,' *understood.*

II. *Attributive adjunct of Subject,* 'all,' *indefinite numeral.*

III. *Predicate,* 'are praising.'

IV. *Object,* 'that,' *restrictive relative.*

15. All controversies that can never end, had better perhaps never begin.

COMPLEX SENTENCE.—A + *a.*

I. *Subject,* 'controversies.'

II. *Attributive adjuncts of Subject* {
1. 'all,' *indefinite numeral.*
2. 'that can never end,' *adjective clause* (*a*)

III. *Predicate,* 'had.'

IV. *Object,* 'never begin,' *infinitive with adverb.*

VI. *Adverbial adjuncts of Predicate*	1. 'Better,' *adv. of Manner* 2. 'perhaps,' *adv. of Uncertainty*

ANALYSIS OF (*a*).

I. *Subject*, 'that.'

III. *Predicate*	1. *Verb of incomplete predication*, 'can.' 2. *Complement*, 'end,' *infinitive*.
VI. *Adverbial adjunct of Predicate*	'never,' *adverb of Time*.

16. He that fights and runs away
May live to fight another day.

COMPLEX SENTENCE.—A + *a* + *a*A + *a*B.

I. *Subject*, 'he.'

II. *Apposition adjunct of Subject*	'that fights and runs away,' *adjective clause (a)*.
III. *Predicate*	1. *Verb of incomplete predication*, 'may.' 2. *Complement*, 'live,' *infinitive*.
VI. *Adverbial adjunct of Predicate*	'to fight another day,' *gerundial adverbial phrase of purpose, (an infinitive qualified by an adverbial phrase)*.

ANALYSIS OF (*a*).

COMPOUND SENTENCE.—[A] That fights; [B] that runs away. A and B are coupled by the cumulative conjunction 'and.'

ANALYSIS OF *a* A.

I. *Subject*, 'that,' *restrictive relative*.

III. *Predicate*, 'fights.'

ANALYSIS OF *a* B.

I. *Subject*, 'that.'

III. *Predicate*, 'runs away,' *compound verb.*

Note.—'That fights and runs away,' cannot be called an adjectival adjunct to the pronoun 'he,' but must be parsed as an adjunct in apposition. A Pronoun, having no independent meaning, cannot be either limited or extended by an adjective. (See above, p. 113.)

17. Meanwhile opinion gilds with varying rays
Those painted clouds that beautify our days.

COMPLEX SENTENCE.—A + *a*.

I. *Subject*, 'opinion.'

III. *Predicate*, 'gilds.'

IV. *Object*, 'clouds.'

V. *Attributive adjuncts of Object*
1. 'those,' *demonstrative adj.*
2. 'painted,' *adj. co-ordinate.*
3. 'that beautify our days,' *adjective clause restrictive (a).*

VI. *Adverbial adjuncts of Predicate*
1. 'meanwhile,' *adv. of Time.*
2. 'with varying rays,' *adverbial phrase of Manner.*

ANALYSIS OF (*a*).

I. *Subject*, 'that.'

III. *Predicate*, 'beautify.'

IV. *Object*, 'days.'

V. *Attributive adjunct of Object* — 'our,' *possessive adjective.*

18. How France was saved from this humiliation, and how the great alliance was preserved, will now be seen.

COMPLEX CONTRACTED SENTENCE.—A + *a* + B + *b*. [A] How France was saved from this humiliation (will now be seen); [B] how the great alliance was preserved, will now be seen. A and B are united by 'and.'

ANALYSIS OF A.

I. *Subject*, 'how France was saved from this humiliation,' *noun clause* (*a*).

III. *Predicate*, 'will be seen.'

VI. *Adverbial adjunct of Predicate*, 'now,' *adv. of Time.*

ANALYSIS OF (*a*).

I. *Subject*, 'France.'

III. *Predicate*, 'was saved.'

VI. *Adverbial adjuncts of Predicate* { 1. 'how,' *adv. of Manner.* 2. 'from this humiliation,' *adv. phrase of place (metaphorical)*

ANALYSIS OF B.

I. *Subject*, 'how the great alliance was preserved,' *noun clause* (*b*).

III. *Predicate*, 'will be seen.'

VI. *Adverbial adjunct of Predicate*, 'now,' *adv. of Time.*

ANALYSIS OF (*b*).

I. *Subject*, 'alliance.'

II. *Attributive adjuncts of Subject* { 'the.' 'great,' *adj. co-ordinate.*

III. *Predicate*, 'was preserved.'

VI. *Adverbial adjunct of Predicate*, 'how.'

19. She loved me for the dangers I had passed.

COMPLEX SENTENCE.—A + a.

I. *Subject,* 'she.'

III. *Predicate,* 'loved.'

IV. *Object,* 'me.'

VI. *Adverbial adjuncts of Predicate* { 'for the dangers I had passed,' *adv. phrase of Cause,* preposition and noun with adjective clause (*a*).

ANALYSIS OF (*a*).

I. *Subject,* 'I.'

III. *Predicate,* 'had passed.'

[IV. *Object,* 'that' *understood.*]

20. The forms of a free constitution surviving when its spirit is extinct, would perpetuate slavery by rendering it more concealed and secure.

COMPLEX SENTENCE.—A + *a*.

I. *Subject,* 'forms.'

II. *Attributive adjuncts of Subject* {
1. 'the.'
2. 'of a free constitution,' *adjective phrase restrictive.*
3. 'surviving when its spirit is extinct,' *participal adjective phrase co-ordinate,* a participle with a qualifying adverbial clause (*a*).

III. *Predicate,* 'would perpetuate.'

IV. *Object,* 'slavery.'

VI. *Adverbial adjunct of Predicate*	'by rendering it more concealed and secure,' *adv. phrase of Cause.*

ANALYSIS OF (*a*).

I. *Subject*, 'spirit.'

II. *Attributive adjunct of Subject*	'its,' *possessive case of pronoun.*
III. *Predicate*	*Verb of incom. predication*, 'is.' *Complement*, 'extinct.'

VI.—*Adverbial adjunct of Predicate*, 'when.'

21. Disquieted by imaginary alarms, insensible to the real danger that awaits them, people are taught to court that servitude which will be a source of misery to themselves and to posterity.

COMPLEX SENTENCE.—$A + a_1 + a_2 + a_2 A + a_2 B$.

I. *Subject*, 'people.'

II. *Attributive adjuncts of Subject*	1. 'disquieted by &c.,' *participial adjective phrase, co-ordinate.* 2. 'insensible to the real danger that awaits them,' *part. adj. phrase, co-ordinate,* comprising adjective clause (a_1).
III. *Predicate*	1. *Verb of incomplete predication*, 'are taught.' 2. *Complement*, 'to court that servitude which &c.,' *infinitive with object and adjuncts,* comprising adjective clause (a_2).

ANALYSIS OF (a^1).

I. *Subject*, 'that.'
III. *Predicate*, 'awaits.'
IV. *Object*, 'them.'

ANALYSIS OF (a_2).

COMPOUND CONTRACTED SENTENCE.—[A] which will be a source of misery to themselves; [B] (which will be a source of misery) to posterity. Conjunction, 'and,' cumulative.

ANALYSIS OF a_2 A.

I. *Subject*, 'which,' improperly used for restrictive 'that.'

III. *Predicate*
1. *Verb of incomplete predication*, 'will be.'
2. *Complement*, 'a source of misery to themselves,' *noun with adjuncts*.

ANALYSIS OF a_2 B.

Exactly like A, except that the Complement is 'a source of misery *to posterity*.'

22. It is only by the fresh feelings of the heart that mankind can be very powerfully affected.

COMPLEX SENTENCE.—A + *a*.

I. *Subject*, 'it.'
II. *Noun clause in apposition to Subject* — 'that mankind can be very powerfully affected,' (*a*).
III. *Predicate*, 'is' (*exists*).
VI. *Adverbial adjuncts of Predicate*
1. 'only,' *adverb of Degree*.
2. 'by the fresh feelings of the heart,' *adv. phrase of Cause*.

ANALYSIS OF (*a*).

I. *Subject*, 'mankind.'

III. *Predicate*	1. *Verb of incomplete predication*, 'can.' 2. *Complement*, 'be affected,' *infinitive.*
VI. *Adverbial adjunct of redicate*	'very powerfully,' *adv. of Manner qualified by adv. of Degree.*

23. Long and various experience seems to have convinced the nations of Europe that nothing but a standing army can oppose a standing army.

COMPLEX SENTENCE.—A + *a*.

I. *Subj ect*, 'experience.'

II. *Attributive adjuncts of Subject.*	'long and various', *adjectives, restrictive.*
III. *Predicate*	1. *Verb of incomplete predication* 'seems.' 2. *Complement*, 'to have convinced the nations of Europe that nothing but a standing army can oppose a standing army,' *infinitive with object and noun clause* (*a*) *as complement.*

ANALYSIS OF (*a*).

I. *Subject*, 'thing.'

II. *Attributive adjunct of Subject*	'no but a standing army,' *adjective qualified by adverbial phrase.*

III. *Predicate*
- 1. *Verb of incomplete predication,* 'can.'
- 2. *Complement,* 'oppose,' *infinitive.*

IV. *Object,* 'army.'

V. *Attributive adjuncts of object*
- 1. 'a.'
- 2. 'standing,' *adjective, restrictive.*

Note.—One way of parsing such verbs as 'taught,' 'convinced,' &c., which take a double object, is to treat one of the objects as a completion of the verb. This is the only correct way when these verbs, as in No. 21, are used in the passive voice. Another way of parsing them is explained in the Grammar, p. 78.

24. In working well, if travail you sustain,
Into the wind shall lightly pass the pain,
But of the deed the glory shall remain.

Compound Complex Contracted Sentence.—A + *a* + B + *b*.—[A] In working well if travail you sustain, into the wind shall lightly pass the pain; [B] in working well if travail you sustain, of the deed the glory shall remain. A and B are opposed by the adversative arrestive conjunction 'but.'

Analysis of A.

I. *Subject* 'pain.'

II. *Attributive adjunct of subject,* 'the.'

III. *Predicate,* 'shall pass.'

VI. *Adverbial adjuncts of Predicate*	1. 'lightly,' *adverb of Manner.* 2. 'into the wind,' *adverbial phrase of place.* 3. 'in working well, if travail you sustain,' *adv. clause of Cause (or Condition) (a).*

ANALYSIS OF (*a*).

I. *Subject,* 'you.'
III. *Predicate,* 'sustain.'
IV. *Object,* 'travail.'

VI. *Adverbial adjunct of Predicate*	'in working well,' *Adv. phrase of Place (metaphorical).*

ANALYSIS OF B.

I. *Subject,* 'glory.'

II. *Attributive adjuncts of Subject*	1. 'the.' 2. 'of the deed,' *prepositional adjective phrase.*

III. *Predicate,* 'shall remain.'

VI. *Adverbial adjunct of Predicate*	'in working well, if travail you sustain,' *adv. clause of Cause (b).*

ANALYSIS OF (*b*).

Same as analysis of (*a*).

25. To prove my assertion we have but to observe what generally passes between the winner and the loser.

COMPLEX SENTENCE.—A + *a*.

I. *Subject,* 'we.'

III. *Predicate*
- 1. *Verb of incomplete predication*, 'have.'
- 2. *Complement*, 'but to observe what generally &c.,' *infinitive enlarged* (1) *by adverb* 'but,' (2) *by noun clause (a) as object*.

VI. *Adverbial adjunct of Predicate* — 'to prove my assertion,' *gerundial adverbial phrase of Cause (or purpose)*.

ANALYSIS OF (*a*).

I. *Subject*, 'what.'
III. *Predicate*, 'passes.'
VI. *Adverbial adjuncts of Predicate*
- 1. 'generally,' *adv. of Time*.
- 2. 'between the winner and the loser,' *adv. phrase of Place (metaphorical)*.

26. Go into Turkey, where the Pachas will tell you that the Turkish government is the most perfect in the world.

COMPOUND SENTENCE.—A + B + *b*. [A] Go into Turkey; [B] there the Pachas will tell you that the Turkish, &c. A and B are united by the co-ordinating relative 'where,' equivalent to 'and there.'

ANALYSIS OF A.

[I. *Subject*, 'you,' *understood*.]
III. *Predicate*, 'go.'
VI. *Adverbial adjunct of Predicate* — 'into Turkey,' *adv. phrase of Place*.

ANALYSIS OF B.

I. *Subject*, 'Pachas.'

II. *Attributive adjunct of Subject*, 'the.'

III. *Predicate*, 'will tell.'

IV. *Object* { 'that the Turkish government, &c.,' *noun clause* (*b*).

VI. *Adverbial adjunct of Predicate* { '(to) you,' *adv. phrase of Place* (*metaphorical*).

Otherwise, the noun clause may be regarded as the complement of 'tell,' and 'you' as the object.

ANALYSIS OF (*b*).

I. *Subject*, 'government.'

II. *Attributive adjuncts of Subject* { 1. 'the.' 2. 'Turkish,' *adj. restrictive*.

III. *Predicate* { 1. *Verb of incomplete predication*, 'is.' 2. *Complement*, 'the most perfect in the world,' *adjective with adverb and adv. phrase of Degree*.

27. All that he does is to distribute what others produce; which is the least part of the business.

COMPOUND SENTENCE.—$A + a_1 + a_2 + B$. [A] All that he does is to distribute what others produce; [B] this is the least part of the business. A and B are united by the co-ordinating relative 'which.'

ANALYSIS OF A.

I. *Subject*, 'business' (or some such word) understood.

II. *Attributive adjuncts of Subject* { 1. 'all,' *indefinite numeral*. 2. 'that he does,' *adjective clause, restrictive* (a_1).

III. *Predicate*
- 1. *Verb of incomplete predication* 'is.'
- 2. *Complement,* 'to distribute what others produce,' *infinitive, with noun clause* (a_2) *as object.*

ANALYSIS OF (a_1).

I. *Subject,* 'he.'
III. *Predicate,* 'does.'
IV. *Object,* 'that,' *restrictive relative.*

ANALYSIS OF (a_2).

I. *Subject,* 'others.'
III. *Predicate,* 'produce.'
IV. *Object,* 'what.'

ANALYSIS OF B.

Subject, 'which,' *co-ordinating relative.*

III. *Predicate*
- 1. *Verb of incomplete predication,* 'is.'
- 2 *Complement,* 'the least part of the business,' *noun with adjuncts.*

28. And even while fashion's brightest arts decoy,
The heart distrusting asks if this be joy.

COMPLEX SENTENCE.—A + a_1 + a_2.

I. *Subject,* 'heart.'

II. *Attributive adjuncts of Subject.*
- 1. 'the.'
- 2. 'distrusting,' *co-ordinate participle.*

III. *Predicate*, asks.'

IV. *Object*, 'if this be joy,' *noun clause* (a_1).

VI. *Attributive adjunct of Predicate* { 'even while fashions's brightest arts decoy,' *adv. clause* (a_2) *of Time, qualified by adv. of Degree* 'even.'

ANALYSIS OF (a_1).

I. *Subject*, 'this.'

III. *Predicate* { 1. *Verb of incomplete predication*, 'be.' 2. *Complement*, 'joy.'

ANALYSIS OF (a_2).

I. *Subject*, 'arts.'

II. *Attributive adjuncts of Subject* { 1. 'fashion's,' *possessive case*. 2. 'brightest,' *restrictive in superlative degree.*

III. *Predicate*, 'decoy.'

VI. *Attributive adjunct of Predicate* { 'while,' *adverb of Time.*

29. Those poets who owe their best fame to his skill
Shall still be his flatterers, go where he will.

COMPLEX SENTENCE.—A + a_1 + a_2.

I. *Subject*, 'poets.'

II. *Attributive adjuncts of Predicate*	1. 'those,' *demonstrative adj.* 2. 'who owe their best fame to his skill,' *restrictive adj. clause* (a_1) ('who' improperly used for 'that').
III. *Predicate*	1. *Verb of incomplete predication*, 'shall.' 2. *Complement*, 'be his flatterers,' *infinitive of incomplete verb with complement*
VI. *Attributive adjuncts of Predicate*	1. 'still,' *adv. of Time.* 2. 'go where he will,' *adv. clause of Place* (a_2).

ANALYSIS OF (a_1).

I. *Subject*, 'who.'	
III. *Predicate*, 'owe.'	
IV. *Object*, 'fame.'	
V. *Attributive adjuncts of Object*	1. 'their,' *possessive adj.* 2. 'best,' *restrictive adjective in superlative Degree.*
VI. *Adverbial adjunct of Predicate*	'to his skill,' *adverbial phrase of Cause.*

ANALYSIS OF (a_2).

I. *Subject*, 'he.'	
III. *Predicate*	1. *Verb of incomplete predication*, 'will.' 2. *Complement*, 'go,' *infinitive.*
VI. *Adverbial adjunct of Predicate*	'where, *adverb of place.*

30. The heart of man craves for sympathy, and each of us seeks a recognition of his talents and his labours.

COMPOUND SENTENCE.—A + B. [A] The heart of man craves for sympathy; [B] each of us seeks a recognition of his talents and his labours. A and B are united by 'and.'

ANALYSIS OF A.

I. *Subject*, 'heart.'

II. *Attributive adjuncts of Subject* { 1. 'the.' 2. 'of man,' *restrictive adj. phrase.*

III. *Predicate*, 'craves.'

VI. *Adverbial adjunct of Predicate* { 'for sympathy,' *adv. phrase of Cause.*

ANALYSIS OF B.

I. *Subject*, 'man' understood.

II. *Attributive adjuncts of Subject* { 1. 'each,' *distributive numeral adj.* 2. 'of us,' *restrictive adj. phrase*

III. *Predicate*, 'seeks.'

IV. *Object*, 'recognition.'

V. *Attributive adjuncts of Object* { 1. 'a.' 2. 'of his talents and his labours,' *restr. adj. phrase.*

Note.—'Craves for' might be taken as a compound verb, with 'sympathy' as object. 'Of us' is formally restrictive, but not really so, 'men' and 'us' being in this case co-extensive. 'Of his talents and of his labours' might be expanded so as to make of B a second compound sentence—

'Each of us seeks a recognition of his talents, and (each of us seeks a recognition of) his labours.'

31. The Dutch florist that sells tulip bulbs for their weight in gold, laughs at the antiquary that pays a great price for a rusty lamp.

COMPLEX SENTENCE.—A + a_1 + a_2

I. *Subject*, 'florist.'

II. *Attributive adjuncts of Subject*
1. 'the.'
2. 'Dutch,' *restrictive adj.*
3. 'that sells tulip bulbs for their weight in gold,' *restrictive adj. phrase* (a_1).

III. *Predicate*, 'laughs at, *compound verb.*

IV. *Object*, 'antiquary.'

V. *Attributive adjuncts of object*
1. 'the.'
2. 'that pays a great price for a rusty lamp,' *restrictive adj. phrase* (a_2).

ANALYSIS OF (a_1).

I. *Subject*, 'that,' *restrictive relative.*

III. *Predicate*, 'sells.'

IV. *Object*, 'bulbs.'

V. *Attributive adjunct of subject* — 'tulip,' *noun used as adjective.*

VI. *Adverbial adjunct of Predicate* — 'for their weight in gold,' *adv. phrase of Cause.*

ANALYSIS OF (a_2).

I. *Subject*, 'that,' *restrictive relative.*

III. *Predicate*, 'pays.'

IV. *Object*, 'price.'

V. *Attributive adjuncts of Object* { 1. 'a.' 2. 'great,' *restrictive adj.*

VI. *Adverbial adjunct of Predicate* { 'for a rusty lamp,' *adv. phrase of Cause.*

32. Here Cumberland lies, having acted his parts,
The Terence of England, the mender of hearts;
A flattering painter, who made it his care
To draw men as they ought to be, not as they are.

COMPLEX SENTENCE.—$A + a + aA + aa + aB + ab$.

Subject, 'Cumberland.'

II. *Attributive adjuncts of Subject.* {
1. 'having acted his parts,' *co-ordinate participial phrase.*
2. 'the Terence of England,' *noun with adjuncts in apposition.*
3. 'the mender of hearts,' *noun with adjuncts in apposition.*
4. 'a flattering painter who made it, &c.,' *noun in apposition with an adj. clause* (*a*) *among its adjuncts.*

III. *Predicate,* 'lies.'

VI. *Adverbial adjunct of Predicate,* 'here,' *adv. of Place.*

ANALYSIS OF (*a*).

COMPOUND CONTRACTED COMPLEX SENTENCE.—[A] Who made it his care to draw men as they ought to be; [B] (who made it) not (his care to draw men) as they are.

ANALYSIS OF *a* A.

I. *Subject,* 'who.'

III. *Predicate* { 1. *Verb of incomplete predication*, 'made.' 2. *Complement*, 'his care.' }

IV. *Object*, 'it.'

V. *Infinitive in apposition to object* { 'to draw men as they ought to be,' *infinitive enlarged* (1) *by obj.* (2) *by adv. clause* (*a a*). }

ANALYSIS OF (*a a*).

I. *Subject*, 'they.'

III. *Predicate* { 1. *Verb of incomplete predication*, 'ought.' 2. *Complement*, 'to be.' }

VI. *Adverbial adjunct of Predicate* { 'as,' *adverb of Manner*. }

ANALYSIS OF *a* B.

I. *Subject*, 'who.'

III. *Predicate* { 1. *Verb of incomplete predication*, 'made not.' 2. *Complement*, 'his care.' }

IV. *Object*, 'it.'

V. *Infinitive in apposition to object* { 'to draw men as they are,' *infinitive enlarged* (1) *by object*, (2) *by adv. clause* (*a b*). }

ANALYSIS OF *a b*.

I. *Subject*, 'they.'

III. *Predicate*, 'are' (exist).

VI. *Adverbial adjunct of Predicate* { 'as,' *adv. of Manner*. }

33. Nor second he that rode sublime
Upon the seraph wings of ecstasy
The secrets of the abyss to spy

COMPLEX SENTENCE.—A + *a*.

I. *Subject*, 'he.'
II. *Apposition adjunct of Subject* { 'that rode sublime upon &c.' (*a*).
III. *Predicate* { 1. *Verb of incomplete predication*, 'was.' 2. *Complement*, 'second.'

ANALYSIS OF (*a*).

I. *Subject*, 'that.'
III. *Predicate*, 'rode.'
VI. *Adverbial adjuncts of Predicate* {
1. 'sublime,' *adj. used by poetical license as adv. of Place.*
2. 'upon the seraph wings of ecstasy,' *adv. phrase of Place (metaphorical).*
3. 'the secrets of the abyss to spy,' *gerundial adv. phrase of Cause.*

34. When civil dudgeon first grew high
And men fell out, they knew not why;
Then did Sir Knight abandon dwelling,
And out he rode a-colonelling.

DOUBLE COMPOUND SENTENCE.—$A_1 + A_1\,a + A_2 + A_2\,a + A_2\,a\,a + B_1 + B_1\,a + B_2 + B_2\,a + B_2\,a\,a$.—[$A_1$] When civil dudgeon first grew high, then did Sir Knight abandon dwelling; [A_2] when men fell out, they knew not why (then did Sir Knight abandon dwelling); [B_1] When civil dudgeon first grew high, (then) out he rode a-colonelling; [B_2] (When men fell out, they knew not why, then) out he rode a-colonelling.

Analysis of A_1.

I. *Subject*, 'Sir Knight,' *compound singular name.*
III. *Predicate*, 'did abandon.'
IV. *Object*, 'dwelling.'
VI. *Adverbial adjunct of Predicate*
 1. 'then,' *adverb of Time.*
 2. when civil dudgeon first grew high, *adverbial clause of Time* (A_1 *a*).

Analysis of A_1 *a*.

I. *Subject*, 'dudgeon.'
V. *Attributive adjunct of subject* — 'civil,' *restrictive adjective.*
III. *Predicate*
 1. *Verb of incomplete predication*, 'grew.'
 2. *Complement*, 'high.'
VI. *Adverbial adjuncts of Predicate*
 1. 'when,' *adverb of Time.*
 2. 'first,' *adverb of Time.*

Analysis of A_2.

I. *Subject*, 'Sir Knight,' *compound Singular name.*
II. *Predicate*, 'did abandon.'
IV. *Object*, 'dwelling.'
VI. *Adverbial adjuncts of Predicate*
 1. 'then,' *adverb of Time.*
 2. 'when men fell out, they knew not why,' *adverbial clause of Time* (A_2 *a*).

Analysis of A_2 *a*.

I. *Subject*, 'men.'
III. *Predicate*, 'fell out,' *compound verb.*
VI. *Adverbial adjuncts of Predicate*
 1. 'when,' *adverb of Time.*
 2. 'they knew not why,' *adv. clause of Manner* (A_2 *a*).

ANALYSIS OF A_2 *a a*.

I. *Subject* 'they.'

III. *Predicate*, 'knew not.'

VI. *Adverbial adjunct of Predicate* { 'why,' *adverb of Manner*.

ANALYSIS OF B_1.

I. *Subject*, 'he.'

III. *Predicate*, 'rode out,' compound verb.

VI. *Adverbial adjuncts of Predicate*
1. 'then, *adv. of Time*.
2. 'when civil dudgeon first grew high, *adv. clause of Time* (B_1 *a*)
3. 'a-colonelling,' *adv. of Manner*.

B_1 *a* is identical with A_1 *a* already analysed.

ANALYSIS OF (B_2).

I. *Subject*, 'he.'

III. *Predicate*, 'rode out,' *compound verb*.

VI. *Adverbial adjuncts of Predicate*
1. 'then,' *adv. of Time*.
2. 'when men fell out, they knew not why,' *adv. clause of Time* (B_2 *a*).
3. a-colonelling,' *adv. of Manner*.

B_2 *a* and B_2 *a a* are identical with A_2 *a* and A_2 *a a* already analysed.

Exercise 19—(p. 184).

Errors in Syntax.

I. *Correct form.*—'Their nature, tempers, qualities, actions, and way, of living were made up of innumerable contradictions.'

'Both' applies only to two things: it cannot be applied, as here, to more than two. 'Was,' after a plural subject, is a breach of the first rule of Concord.—The sentence is from Defoe, whose grammar is often at fault.

2. *Correct form.*—'Scotland and thou did in each other live.'

'Thee' is wrong: the subject of a verb should be in the Nominative case.

3. *Correct form.*—'O thou for ever present in my way,
Who all my motives and my toils survey*est.*'

Correct grammar here mars the rhyme. 'Survey' should be 'surveyest:' the rule being that the relative takes the 'person' of the antecedent.

4. *Correct form.*—'I had written to him the day before.'

'Wrote' should be 'written' (Gram. p. 180). It is the perfect participle, and not the inflected form for the past tense, that is used in making up the past perfect.

5. *Correct form.*—'The reason of his attending their meetings was simply that he wished to obstruct them.'

'Him' should be 'his.' 'Him' is here an infringement of the second rule of government (Gram. p. 181): 'attending' is an infinitive, not a participle. 'Were' should be 'was,' after a singular subject—'reason.' 'Wishes' should be 'wished,' according to the rule for the Concord of Tenses: the principal tense 'was' being past, the subordinate tense 'wished' must be past also.

6. *Correct form.*—'The rise and fall of nations is an interesting study.'

'Are' should be 'is:' 'rise' and 'fall' are two nouns united by 'and,' but they make a single compound subject by their union.

7. *Correct form.*—'Great pains was taken to avoid such a calamity.'

'Were' should be 'was:' 'pains' is plural in form, but it is a singular noun, and must be followed by a singular verb. 'To have avoided,' should be to 'avoid:' the perfect infinitive (Gram. p. 180) should not be used after a past tense.

8. *Correct form.*—'The mind and the body remain invincible.'

'The' should be repeated before 'body,' 'mind' and 'body' being two different subjects (Gram. p. 182). For the same reason 'remains' should be 'remain.'

9. *Correct form.*—'The fact of my going away could not signify.'

Cp No. 5.—'Going away' is an infinitive, and should not be preceded by an objective. A possessive adjective serves the same purpose as the possessive case of a pronoun.

10. *Correct form.*—'Nor want nor cold his course delays.'

The conjunction being alternative, and 'want' and 'cold' both singular, the verb must be singular.

11. *Correct form.*—'She fell a-laughing, like one out of her right senses;' or, more politely, 'out of one's right senses.'

Many good writers use 'their' after a singular indefinite pronoun, but here the incongruity of number is too glaring. To the possessive adjective 'her' it may be objected that the gender of 'one,' which the adjective is in concord with, is not necessarily feminine: she laughed like any person, *man* or woman out of *his* or her right senses. Perhaps 'one's' is the safest word to use, though it is a little stiff.

12. *Correct form.*—'There is a class of men that never look before their noses.'

'Are' should probably be 'is:' the collective noun 'class' being here used for an aggregate, or body of individuals taken all together. 'Looks' should be 'look;' the antecedent of the relative being 'men,' not 'class,' and the rule being that the antecedent regulates the number of the relative.

'Who,' the relative of co-ordination, is here out of place. The clause is restrictive, and the relative should be 'that.'

13. *Correct form.*—'I, your friend, advise you not to trust any of the three partners.'

'Advises' should be 'advise': 'I,' not 'friend,' is the subject of the verb. 'Your friend,' is an abbreviated co-ordinate clause, equivalent to 'who am your friend.' 'Either' is one of *two*, not one of *three*: 'any' is the proper adjective when there are more than two.

14. *Correct form.*—'Between you and me, there were various causes at work.'

'I' should be in the objective case, after the proposition 'between.' 'Variety' being used with the indefinite article, 'a' is grammatically singular, and 'was' is formally correct. But the sense is plural, and demands a plural verb. The best course in such cases is to avoid the awkward construction, and use an equivalent expression.

15. *Correct form.*- 'The only real hindrance to its being attainable, is the wonderfully imprudent character of the people.'

Cp. 5, 9. 'Being attainable' is an infinitive, and should be preceded by the possessive 'its.' 'Wonderful' is an adjective improperly used for an adverb.

16. *Correct form.*—'Though four-fifths of the population are Celtic and Roman Catholic, more than four-fifths of the property belongs to Protestants.'

'Is' should be 'are.' The abstract noun 'four-fifths' in the first clause is used as a collective noun distributively; so many of the population are spoken of individually as regards their religious beliefs. 'Belong' should be 'belongs.' 'Four-fifths' in the second clause is used as a collective noun of heterogeneous material (see above, Exercise 6, No. 4, p. 22), and requires a singular verb. These abstract expressions for fractions take on the character of the noun that they are used with: the number of the verb, as a rule, is regulated by the number of that noun.

17. *Correct form.*—'No other river such fine salmon feeds.'

'Feed' should be 'feeds.' This is an example of the ear being perverted by an intervening prominent noun of different number (Gram. p. 177).

18. *Correct form.*—'The books were laid upon the table.'

'Lain' should be 'laid.' 'Lain' is the perfect participle of the intransitive verb 'lie,' not of the transitive verb 'lay.' The conjugation of 'lie' is 'lie, lay, lain;' of 'lay'—'lay, laid, laid.'

19. *Correct form.*—'He is one of the best and wisest men that have ever lived.'

'Has ever lived' is wrong: the antecedent of the relative is the plural 'men,' not the singular 'one.'

'Who' is not the proper relative: the clause is restrictive, and should be introduced by 'that.'

20. *Correct form.*—'He trusted to equal the Most High.'

Cp. 7. It is incorrect to use the perfect infinitive after a past tense.

21. *Correct form.*—'Every tub must stand upon its own bottom.'

'Their' is wrong: 'every tub' is singular (Gram. p. 179).

22. *Correct form.*—'That is the man that I perceived to be in fault.'

'Was' must be made 'to be:' it is the function of the infinitive to name an action in the manner of a noun: the third person singular of a tense cannot stand as the object of a verb. 'Being in fault,' the state expressed by this complex verb, either is the object of 'perceived'—'that,' the secondary object, being considered equivalent to 'in the case of whom,' and so equivalent to an adverbial phrase: or it may be regarded as the completion of 'perceived.' (See above, p. 32).

The clause being restrictive, 'that' is preferable to 'whom.'

23. *Correct form.*—'You are the first to rear your head.'

We can see from the meaning and from the use of 'your' in the relative clause that the antecedent intended is 'you.' This, however, is awkward, as we naturally refer the relative to 'the first (person).' 'The first to rear your head' is the idiomatic construction. The infinitive 'to rear' is explained by supposing the omission of a preposition, such as 'as regards:' 'you are the first as regards rearing (to rear) your head.'

24. *Correct form.*—'His Elements of Political Economy was very favourably reviewed.'

'Were' is wrong: 'Elements of Political Economy,' though the leading noun is plural, is a singular name, being the title of a book, and requires a singular verb (Gram. p. 178).

25. *Correct form.*—'The play is most perniciously slow.'

Cp. 15.

26. *Correct form.*—'The tenantry have resolved to celebrate the marriage of their young proprietor with all the honours.'

The tenants, though coming to the resolution collectively, are supposed to act individually, and therefore 'tenantry' is followed by a plural noun. To avoid the clash of a nominative singular in form and a verb plural in form, many writers would prefer using the plural of the class noun 'tenants.'

27. *Correct form.*—'All the human race would fain be wits;' or 'All men would fain be wits.'

It is not idiomatic to use 'all' alone with a collective noun: we must put in 'the.'

The second form is perhaps preferable for the same reason that would make us write 'tenants' in place of 'tenantry' in No. 26. There is a collision in form between the singular 'race' and the plural 'wits' applying to the same subject.

28. *Correct form.*—'Each makes as much profit as he can.'

'Make' is decidedly wrong: 'each' is singular and requires a singular verb. 'They,' however, might stand, did it not come so soon and so prominently after the singular verb. Many good writers use a plural pronoun to refer to 'each' for the reason given in Grammar, p. 179: 'each' is common gender, and there is no corresponding singular pronoun of common gender.

29. *Correct form.*—'Sir William Temple had a good shape, and was extremely active.'

'Extreme,' misused for extremely. Cp. Nos. 15, 25.

30. *Correct form.*—'His honourable and amiable disposition was praised by everybody.'

This is an example of the misleading effect of the two adjectives coupled by 'and' upon the number of the verb.

31. *Correct form.*—'Shattered by the fever, he was left by his friends to his fate.'

A participial phrase standing at the beginning of the sentence applies to the subject (Gram. p. 160): and it being 'he' and not 'his friends' that are meant to have been shattered, we must alter the sentence so as to make 'he' the subject. Another way of correcting the bad grammar, would be to insert 'as he was,' thus—'Shattered as he was by the fever, his friends &c.'

32. *Correct form.*—'I am afraid of the man's dying before a doctor can come.'

The possessive 'man's' is required before the infinitive 'dying.' Cp. No. 15.

33. *Correct form.*—'It was very characteristic of Bacon to say that by indignities men come to dignities.'

'Came' is wrong: Bacon did not mean the expression to apply only to his own time, and the present indefinite (Gram. p. 146) is the tense for propositions applicable to all time.

As another example of this kind of error, reference may be made to Exercise 10, 21 (p. 53)—'the loud laugh that *spoke* the vacant mind.' 'Spoke' should be 'speaks:' the writer did not mean that this sort of laughter was in his time a thing of the past: he intended a proposition true of all times, and should have used the indefinite universal tense.

34. *Correct form.*—'If we could only hold our tongues, everything would succeed to perfection.'

Either 'could' or 'will' must be changed, to preserve concord between the principal and the subordinate clauses.

'To a wish,' though significant enough, is a Scotch idiom.

35. *Correct form.*—'He has not sufficient wages to support a growing family.'

'Wages,' though plural in form, is singular in meaning, and should in strictness be followed by a singular verb. At the same time, a noun of plural form coming immediately before a verb of singular form, has a very awkward sound. The best course is to evade the construction by some such alternative as the above.

36. *Correct form.*—'Have you seen the minister and the schoolmaster to-day.'

'The minister and schoolmaster' is allowable only if both the offices are held by the same man, and the two nouns apply to the same person. If two different persons are denoted, the article must be repeated (Gram. p. 182).

'The day' is a Scotticism for 'to-day.'

37. *Correct form.*—'The bliss that centres only in the mind.'

The relative clause being restrictive, 'that' is preferable to 'which.' 'The' may be substituted for 'that' to avoid the recurrence of *that*. 'Only,' in the original form is misplaced. When put between 'which' and 'centres,' it naturally is taken to qualify either the one or the other. If it qualifies 'which,' the meaning is—'the *only* bliss that centres in the mind,' implying that there is but one bliss that does so centre. If it qualifies 'centres,' the meaning is—'the bliss that only *centres*,' and does nothing else that it might be expected to do. But we know that neither of these meanings is the meaning intended by the poet (GOLDSMITH, *Traveller*). He means the bliss that is not to be found in one country more than in another, 'the bliss that centres only *in the mind*.'

> Vain, very vain, my weary search to find
> The bliss that centres only in the mind.

38. *Correct form.*—'We should make a great mistake if we supposed wealth and rank exempt from care and toil.'

'We would' is a wrong inflection: 'we should' is the proper inflection for conditional futurity. The inflection of the plural is 'We should, you would, they would.' 'Be mistaken,' in this sense, is a bad idiom: we must use another construction. 'Suppose' does not concord with the past tense in the principal clause.

39. *Correct form.*—'Hoping to hear from you soon, I am, believe me, yours truly.'

Cp. No. 31. The participial clause intended to apply to the writer, would apply to the person addressed, the subject of the principal verb 'believe.' We must contrive a sentence that shall have 'I' as its subject.

40. *Correct form.*—'He was a plague to his parents at home, and the master could make almost nothing of him at school.'

The introductory participial phrase would apply to the master, the subject of the sentence, not to the boy. The neatest way out of the difficulty is to make the co-ordinate phrase a separate sentence. 'Almost' is misplaced, being put so as to qualify 'make,' instead of 'nothing.'

41. According to the rule laid down under No. 16, this form is correct. The nouns 'miseries' and 'vices' being plural, the fraction is also considered plural. Had 'misery' stood alone—'nine-tenths of the misery of mankind,' then 'nine-tenths' would have been regarded as singular, and the verb would have been 'proceeds.' Were 'misery and vice' used—'nine-tenths of the misery and vice,' then, to carry out our rule strictly, we should have to consider 'nine-tenths' plural, 'misery and vice' together being a plural combination: but in such a case probably the ear is better satisfied with a singular verb.

42. *Correct form.*—'He complained that he had been suffered to use the horse only for one day,' or 'for one day only.'

The pronoun 'he' refers to two different persons, and thereby causes unnecessary confusion (Gram. p. 183). We must make a construction, such as the above, that shall convey the same meaning without intricacy. 'Only' is misplaced: it is intended to qualify, not 'to use,' but 'for one day.'

43. See above, p. 41, ADJECTIVE, Q. 11.

44, 45, 46. *Correct forms.*—'He endeavoured not only to do his duty, but to make others do theirs.'

'Some persons can distinguish only black, white, and gray.'

'This seems to be owing not so much to the want of physical power, but rather to the absence of vehemence.'

See Gram. p. 183. When a verb applies to two clauses, it should not be entangled with any part of the first.

47. *Correct form.*—'The attempt may succeed in this case, but it cannot often be made with safety.'

Cp. No. 42. 'It' has here no less than three different references. The first 'it' refers forward to the clause—'that it is safe to make it;' the second 'it' refers forward to the phrase—'to make it;' and the third refers back to the word 'attempt.' Such perplexity of reference in the same sentence should be avoided by using another construction. 'It' is employed for so many different references that we may not always be able to find a substitute: but we should always try.

ADDITIONAL EXERCISES.

PARSING FOR SYNTAX.

WHEN his classes are asked to parse for Syntax alone, the teacher should be careful to prevent them from parsing with a view to the other divisions of grammar—Parts of Speech, Inflection, or Analysis. So far, indeed, parsing for Syntax presupposes parsing for Parts of Speech and for Inflection. Concord in Syntax means concord or agreement of inflections for number, person, and tense; Government in Syntax means the regulation of the inflection for case: before, therefore, we can parse for Concord or for Government in Syntax, we must have distinguished or 'parsed' the inflections for number, person, tense, and case. Again, the Order of Words in Syntax, means the Order of the Parts of Speech according to what they are—Nouns, Pronouns, Verbs, Adjectives, or Adverbs: before we can say whether or not the rules for the Order of Words have been observed, we must know what Parts of Speech the several words belong to. But in parsing for Concord we take no notice of inflections that are not in concord with other inflections: in parsing for Government, we attend only to Cases and to how they are produced: and in parsing for Order of Words it is enough to know merely the Part of Speech without paying attention to the sub-division.

1. 'My lambkins around me would oftentimes play.' (Exercise 17, 14: p. 152).

Concord.—*Lambkins would play*—a plural subject followed by a plural verb (CONCORD, 2). In this tense the verb has the same inflection for the first and third persons singular, and for the three persons of the plural. Still the verb may be said to be in concord with its subject: the same inflection is used for other persons and the other number, but a different inflection would be inadmissible.

There is no farther concord or agreement of inflection in the sentence.

Government.—'Me' is governed in the objective case by the preposition 'around' (GOVERNMENT, 1).

Order of Words.—In parsing for Order it is well to begin with a general statement as to whether the order is regular or irregular upon the whole. If there is any irregularity, it should be noticed first; and though, in a set exercise, the pupils should notice conformity as well as non-conformity with the rules, it may be sufficient, in hurried parsing, to notice only the irregularities.

In this sentence the adverbial phrase 'around me' is not placed according to the general rule. According to that rule it should come after, not before. It is here put before on account of the metre. Departures from the usual order are often made for the sake of emphasis; but here it is the metre alone that rules the order: 'would oftentimes play around me' is no less emphatic than—'around me would oftentimes play.'

'Oftentimes' is regularly placed between the auxiliary and the verb. The adjective 'my' regularly precedes its noun 'lambkins.'

In this the first example of parsing for Syntax, the teacher should repeat and enforce minutely the difference between parsing for Syntax and parsing for Parts of Speech and for Inflection (parsing for Analysis is a process so markedly different that there is no risk of confounding it with any of the other modes). In parsing for Parts of Speech we should have to say what class of Adjectives 'my' belong to; what class of Nouns 'lambkins' belongs to; what class of Prepositions 'around' belongs to; what class of Pronouns 'me' belongs to; what classes of Adverbs the phrase 'around me' and the word 'oftentimes' belong to; what classes of Verbs 'would' and 'play' belong to. In parsing for Inflection we should have to give the tense and the mood of 'would,' and the mood of 'play.'

The teacher may even make his classes actually parse the sentence for Parts of Speech and for Inflection; repeating the process on other sentences till he has fulfilled the no doubt difficult task, of making the pupils understand the distinction.

2. 'But anxious cares the pensive nymph oppressed' (Exer. 1, 8, p. 72).

Concord.—The inflection of the subject 'cares' corresponds with the inflection of the verb 'oppressed.' The two inflections are, as explained in No. 1, in concord. It may be well, however, as a means of keeping the pupil's attention awake, to make him remark the concord only when the verb as well as the subject has a distinctive inflection for number or person. This happens in the second and the third persons singular of the Present tense, and in the second person singular of the Past tense, Indicative Mood: there is no distinctive inflection either for number or for person in the Subjunctive Mood. The pupil may remark upon the Concord only in those three persons: when the verb is in the first person singular or in any of the three persons of the plural, there is in one sense no concord of inflections, the verb not being distinctively inflected. Where the verb is not distinctively inflected, the pupil should either enter under the head of Concord—'No instance;' or if he does remark upon the Concord, he should point out clearly that the inflection of the verb is not distinctive either for the number or for the person.

Government.—No instance.

Order of Words.—The only irregularity consists in placing the object with its adjuncts—'the pensive nymph'—before the verb. The regular order is departed from for the sake of metre and rhyme.

The adjectives 'anxious' and 'pensive' regularly precede their nouns. The definite article 'the' comes before the other adjective.

3. 'I have a strange infirmity, which is nothing to those that know me' (Exer. 7, 31, p. 55).

Concord.—In 'I have' and 'that know,' the verbs are not distinctively inflected for number or person. In 'which is' and 'that know,' the subjects are not distinctively inflected for number: the pronouns 'which' and 'that' have the same form whether singular or plural in their reference. There is, therefore, in this sentence no decided case of concordant inflections: no case where we can tell the number of both subject and verb from looking at each separately without looking at the other.

The number of 'which' and 'that' is determined by their antecedents—'infirmity' and 'persons' understood—according to the rule (Concord, 7).

The demonstrative adjective 'those' is inflected for number to agree with its noun—'persons,' or some such word, understood.

The tenses 'is,' 'have,' and 'know,' are in Concord.

Government.—The pronoun 'me' is governed in the objective case by the verb 'know.'

Order of Words.—The order is regular. The adjective 'strange' precedes its noun 'infirmity:' the adjective clauses follow their nouns, which is the invariable arrangement.

4. 'Soon will the high midsummer pomps come on' (Exer. 10, 19; p. 72).

Concord.—No instance.

Government.—No instance.

Order of Words.—The order is irregular.

The subject with its adjuncts—'the high midsummer pomps,' is placed between the auxiliary and the verb: whereas, according to the rule that the Subject precedes the Verb, it should come before the auxiliary. The adverb 'soon,' which in regular order follows an intransitive verb, is placed at the very beginning of the sentence. The regular order would be—'The high midsummer pomps will come on soon.' This is departed from for the sake of metre.

5. 'Whether he stops or goes, is to me a matter of indifference' (Exer. 13, 22; p. 109).

Concord.—The inflection of the subject 'he' for number and person corresponds to the inflection of the verbs 'stays' and 'goes' for number and person. The clause 'whether he stays or goes'—the subject of the sentence, being regarded as a singular noun, takes the third person singular of the verb to correspond.

Government.—'Me' is governed in the objective case by the preposition 'to.'

Order of words.—The order, though it does not depart from the primary rules, is not quite usual. The adverbial phrase 'to me' is placed between the substantive verb and its complement: the more usual arrangement would be to place it after the complement, though this arrangement has the advantage of making the application of the adverbial phrase emphatic and unmistakable. It is also more common, though not for any special reason preferable, to begin such a sentence as this with the pronoun 'it,' and to bring in the noun clause, which is the real subject, at the end in apposition to 'it,' thus —'It is a matter of indifference to me whether he goes or stays.'

6. 'Unless you study, you will not become learned' (Exer. 14, 4; p. 110.)

Concord.—The tenses 'study' and 'will' are in concord. '*Would* not become,' would be out of concord.

Government.—No instance.

Order of words.—According to the rule that the adverb follows the Verb, the adverbial clause should follow the principal clause—'You will not become learned, unless you study.' Both arrangements are quite common. When the adverbial adjunct is brought in before the principal verb, the structure is said to be 'periodic': when it is brought in after the principal verb, the structure is said to be 'loose.'

7. But how can he expect that others should
Build for him, sow for him, and at his call
Love him, who for himself will take no heed at all.
(Exer. 15, 3; p. 129).

Concord.—No instance of the concord of distinctive inflections in subject and verb.

The singular number and third person of the relative 'who' are determined by the antecedent 'he.'

The tenses 'expect' and 'will' are in Concord.

Government.—'Build for him,' 'sow for him,' 'for himself;' objectives governed by prepositions. 'Love him,' objective governed by 'love.'

Order of Words.—For the sake of metre, there are a good many departures from the regular order. The relative clause 'who for himself will take no heed at all,' is farther separated from the antecedent 'he' than is permissible in prose style. The adverbial phrase 'at his call,' if intended to qualify all the three predicates 'build for him,' 'sow for him,' and 'love him,' should be placed before the first of them to make its application unmistakable. If intended to qualify 'love him' alone, it is properly placed for the purpose of preventing confusion, but is not placed in accordance with the general rule that in the case of a transitive verb, the adverb follows the object. According to rule, 'for himself' should come after 'at all;' and in this position it would also be best placed for emphasis: it stands where it is for the sake of metre.

It may here be remarked that there is no grammatical error in departing from the general rules for order. In parsing, however, the pupil should be trained to know what the rules are, that he may know not to depart from them without reason. The principles of effective order belong rather to Rhetoric or Composition than to Grammar: but even at this stage, in noting departures from the general rules, the pupils may be gradually and easily made familiar with some of the most important of those principles. The departures that beginners will most readily understand, are departures made for the sake of metre: departures for emphasis and clearness they cannot be expected to understand so readily.

GENERAL PARSING.

One of the chief objections commonly urged against the teaching of grammar to young children is, that almost invariably parsing becomes a matter of rote; that the pupil simply learns to repeat certain forms without attaching any meaning to them, and obtains no intellectual discipline from the exercise. The only way to prevent this is to vary the forms of parsing, and to introduce distinctions that cannot be caught without some effort of thought. It requires very little thought to see the difference between a noun and an adjective, or between a noun and a verb. If grammatical discipline is to teach pupils to think and not merely to repeat, we must introduce nicer distinctions: we must ask them to distinguish classes of Nouns, Verbs, Adjectives, and other Parts of Speech. If it be thought that these distinctions are beyond children, then we must put off the age for beginning grammar, until children are capable of understanding and making these nicer distinctions; teaching them to repeat grammatical rules does no more to quicken their intellects than teaching them to repeat nursery rhymes. While children are not old enough to understand the differences between an Abstract noun and a General noun, between an Indefinite infinitive and a Gerundial infinitive, or between parsing for Parts of Speech and parsing for Inflection, they would perhaps be better employed in committing to memory choice passages of English composition, than in repeating and applying superficial grammatical rules.

One way of ensuring some thought in the exercise of parsing is to parse for each of the four divisions of Grammar —Parts of Speech, Inflection, Analysis, and Syntax—in separation. The teacher may now and then vary this, and take two or three or all of them at the same time. It will stimulate the ingenuity of the apter pupils to the utmost, to make them sometimes parse for Parts of Speech and Inflection alone, sometimes for Parts of Speech and Analysis alone, sometimes for Syntax and Inflection alone, and so on through the other possible combinations. This thorough method of parsing will take longer time than the method commonly practised: but it is much more likely to be of service in awakening the mind, a more important end in education than mere rapidity of glib repetition.

1.

'Laughing to one's self is unpolite in company.'

For Parts of Speech alone.—In this parsing we do not confine ourselves to taking the words singly: we take them in phrases, or combinations, when these play the same part as a single word.

'Laughing,' verb, intransitive.

'To,' preposition of place, *motion with direction* (one of the case-prepositions). Its primary meaning of 'motion towards' can here be easily traced.

'One's,' pronoun, indefinite demonstrative or indefinite personal (see above, p. 30). Here it is a polite substitute for 'your,' helping to give a piece of advice with a less offensive air.

'Self,' noun, abstract.

'One's self,' compound pronoun, reflective; used with the preposition 'to,' in the phrase 'to one's self.'

'To one's self,' adverbial phrase, primarily of place, here merely of manner.

'Is,' verb of incomplete predication.

'Unpolite,' adjective, quality, complement of 'is.'

'In,' preposition, place, *rest in.*

'Company,' noun, usually collective, here employed by a peculiar idiom as an abstract noun; used with the prep. 'in,' in the phrase 'in company.'

'In company,' adverbial phrase of place, *rest in.*

For Inflection alone.—The inflected words are 'laughing,' one's,' and 'is.'

'Laughing,' infinitive indefinite. We know that it is not a participle because it is the subject of the sentence: we know that it is not a verbal noun because it is qualified by an adverbial phrase: we know that it is not a gerundial infinitive because it does not express a purpose.

'One's,' possessive case.

'Is,' indicative mood, present tense, singular number, third person. [The order is here on purpose inverted from the order followed in Exercise 17: such changes are a preventive against repetition by rote. The 'voice' is not mentioned, the verb having but one voice. Similarly, 'indefinite' is omitted, the present tense having but one form.]

For Analysis alone.

I. *Subject*, 'laughing to one's self,' *infinitive with adverbial qualification.*

III. *Predicate*	1. *Verb of incomplete predication*, 'is.' 2. *Complement*, 'unpolite,' *adj.*
VI. *Adverbial adjunct of Predicate*	'in company,' *adverbial phrase.*

In parsing for analysis a passage that is not separately parsed for Parts of Speech also, it is well to make the pupils refer phrases, adjectives, and adverbs to their sub-divisions.

This, however, is to some extent trenching upon parsing for Parts of Speech; and is unnecessary and even incorrect when the parsing is for Analysis alone as distinguished from parsing for Parts of Speech alone.

For Syntax alone. Concord.—There is here no instance of distinctive inflections in concord. 'Laughing,' the subject, being an infinitive, is not inflected for number.

Government.—'One's' is governed in the possessive case by the noun 'self.'

Order of words.—The order is regular. The adverbial phrases 'one's self' and 'in company' follow their verbs.

As the phrase 'in company' stands, it qualifies 'is unpolite.' But the meaning would be brought out more distinctly if it were made to qualify the subject 'laughing to one's self.' In that view the correct order would be—'Laughing to one's self in company is unpolite.'

2.

'What Art does for men, Nature has done for animals, which are themselves incapable of art.' (Exer. 7, 23; p. 36.)

For Parts of Speech and Inflection together.—'What.' We may here take 'what' either as a compound relative equivalent to 'that which,' or (see Gram. p. 162) as an interrogative used indefinitely. If we take it as a compound relative, then we must regard the implied 'that' as the object of 'has done,' 'which,' the other part of 'what,' being the object 'does.' If we take it as an interrogative, we must regard the whole clause 'what art does for men' as a noun clause, object of 'has done.'

'Art,' noun, usually Abstract; here personified, and so Singular or Proper; used as subject of a sentence. It is significant. Cp. 'Chaos' and 'Night,' Exer. 5, 7; p. 20.

'Does' verb, transitive (object—'what' or 'which' according to the view taken of 'what') active voice, indicative mood, present indefinite tense, singular number, third person. An example of the present indefinite used as the *Universal* tense.

'For,' preposition of end, one of the case-prepositions, here used in its meaning of 'benefit.'

'Men,' noun, general and significant, plural number; here used with a preposition is the phrase 'for men.'

'For men,' adverbial phrase of cause.

'Nature,' parsed exactly like 'Art.'

'Has,' auxiliary verb, indicative mood, present tense, singular number, third person: used with 'done' to make up the present perfect tense of the verb 'do.'

'Done,' verb, transitive (object—'that' or 'what art does for men' according to the view taken of 'what'), perfect participle used with 'has' to make up the third person singular present perfect indicative active of the verb 'do.'

'Animals,' noun, general and significant, plural number; here used with a preposition in the phrase 'for animals.' 'Animals' is a higher class than 'men,' comprehending mammals, birds, fishes, insects, &c., as well as 'men.' [Animals is sometimes incorrectly used for the lower animals, that is, for all animals except men, and this would seem to be the meaning intended in the text].

'For animals,' adverbial phrase of cause.

'Which,' pronoun, relative (referring to 'animals'), coordinating. [Unless 'animals' is used in the restricted sense above mentioned, 'which' is not here the proper relative. If 'animals' is used in its wide and correct sense, the relative clause is intended to restrict the class to all animals except men, and should be introduced by the restrictive relative—'that'].

'Themselves,' pronoun, demonstrative, reflective, plural number.

'Incapable,' adjective of quality, complement of 'are.'

'Of,' preposition of reference (one of the case-prepositions). This is evidently an instance of the reference meaning of 'of:' the idea is—'incapable *as regards* art.'

'Art,' noun, abstract, used with a preposition in the phrase 'of art.' In this connection it is not personified.

'Of art,' adverbial phrase of manner *(reference)*.

'Which are themselves incapable of art,' adjective clause, co-ordinate or restrictive, according to the view taken of the meaning of 'animals.'

For Analysis.—A + a_1 + a_2.

I. *Subject*, 'Nature.'

III. *Predicate*, 'has done.'

IV. *Object*, 'what art does for men,' *noun clause* (a_1).

VI. *Adverbial adjuncts of Predicate* { 'for animals which are, &c.' *adverbial phrase containing adjective clause* (a_2).

ANALYSIS OF a_1.

I. *Subject*, 'art.'

III. *Predicate*, 'does.'

IV. *Object*, 'what.'

VI. *Adverbial adjunct of Predicate* { 'for men,' *adverbial phrase.*

ANALYSIS OF a_2.

I. *Subject*, 'which.'

II. *Adjunct of Subject* { 'themselves,' *reflective pronoun in apposition.*

III. *Predicate*	1. *Verb of incomplete predication*, 'are.' 2. *Complement*, 'incapable.'
VI. *Adverbial adjunct of Predicate*	'of art,' *adverbial phrase.*

For Syntax. Concord.—In *Art does*, and *Nature has done*, we have instances of singular inflections in concord.

The relative 'which' takes its number from the antecedent 'animals.'

The tenses 'does,' 'has done,' and 'are,' are in concord.

Government.—No instance.

Order of Words.—The only departure from the general rule is in the position of the object noun clause 'what Art does for men.' The object usually follows the verb; here it is placed before the verb.

The normal order would be—'Nature has done for animals which are themselves incapable of art, what art does for men.' The order in the text is adopted for emphasis: greater attention is drawn to the object clause when it is placed at the beginning out of the usual order.

The adjective clause 'which are' &c., is well placed for the purpose of making unmistakable the reference of 'which' to its antecedent.

3.

'It is hard to say in what department of human thought and endeavour conformity has triumphed most.'

For Parts of Speech, Inflection and Analysis.—In this complex parsing, it is perhaps best to make the analysis the principal operation and the others subsidiary.

COMPLEX SENTENCE.—A + *a*.

A.

I. *Subject*, 'it;' pronoun, demonstrative, singular number, neuter gender; refers forward to II.

II. *Apposition Adjunct of Subject*, 'to say in what department of human thought and endeavour conformity has triumphed most;' infinitive followed by noun clause (*a*).

'To say,' verb, transitive (object—noun clause *a*), infinitive indefinite.

III. *Predicate*. 1. *Verb of incomplete predication*, 'is.' 2. *Complement*, 'hard.'

'Is,' incomplete verb, indicative mood, present tense, singular number, third person.

'Hard,' adjective of quality, complement of 'is.'

a.

I. *Subject*, 'conformity,' noun, abstract, active verbal—equivalent to 'the act of conforming.'

III. *Predicate*, 'has triumphed;' verb, intransitive, indicative mood, present-perfect tense, singular number, third person.

'Has,' auxiliary verb, indicative mood, present tense, singular number, third person.

'Triumphed,' verb, intransitive, perfect participle; used with 'has' to make up the present perfect tense.

VI. *Adverbial Adjuncts of Predicate.*—1. 'Most,' adverb of degree. 2. 'In what department of human thought and endeavour,' adverbial phrase of place (metaphorical).

'In,' preposition of place, rest in.

'What,' being accompanied by a noun, must here be parsed as a pronominal adjective, interrogative indefinite.

'Department,' noun, general and significant. In one view 'department' is abstract, meaning a space portioned or parted off without reference to anything but its being parted off. In this view it is the passive verbal corresponding to the active verbal 'partition.'

'Of,' case-preposition, partitive meaning.

'Human,' adjective of quality.

'Thought,' noun, abstract, active verbal—equivalent to 'the act of thinking.'

'And,' conjunction, co-ordinating, cumulative.

'Endeavour,' noun, abstract, active verbal—equivalent to 'the act of endeavouring.'

For Syntax.—Concord.—'It is,' and 'conformity has,' are examples of the concord of inflections for singular number. In both cases we can tell the number of the one part of speech without looking to the other.

Government.—No instance.

Order of Words.—Regular.—'It' refers forward to an infinitive, and there is nothing to make the reference indistinct.

4.

'To the south of Asia lies the group of the Sundas with its thousand islands and islets.'

For Parts of Speech, Inflection and Syntax.—As a rule it is well to keep the parsing for Syntax distinct; but occasionally, as an exercise of the ingenuity, it may be taken along with the other modes.

'To,' preposition of place, placeand direction.

'The,' demonstrative adjective or definite article. Here it has no special limiting force, and is, indeed, almost superfluous.

'South,' noun, abstract, with corresponding adjective 'southern;' used with a preposition in a phrase.

'Of,' preposition of place, expressing place and direction. There is here a distinct remainder of its primary meaning 'proceeding from'—'south *proceeding from* Asia.' 'South *from* Asia' is another recognised form of the phrase.

'Asia,' noun, proper (singular and meaningless). 'Asia' is purely Singular: when used alone, it suggests the continent so called and nothing else. When applied to any other place it is enlarged by an adjective, as in Asia Minor (Asia the Less), and Australasia (Southern Asia).

'To the south of Asia,' adverbial phrase of place, placeand direction. Contrary to the general rule that the adverb follows theverb, this phrase is placed before its verb. It is so placed for the sake of clearness and emphasis.

'Lies,' verb, intransitive, indicative mood, present indefinite tense, singular number, third person. It is in concord with the singular subject 'group.'

'The,' has here a decided limiting force, pointing to one particular group.

'Group,' noun, collective; used as the subject of a sentence. Contrary to the general rule that the subject precedes the verb, it is placed after the verb. The phrase 'to the south of Asia' being placed at the beginning, 'the group' must come after the verb, otherwise it would be unduly separated either from the verb 'lies,' or from its adjuncts 'of the Sundas &c.'

'Of,' here case-preposition, reference meaning, or simply preposition of reference.

'The' has more limiting force than in the first case, and less than in the second.

'Sundas,' a meaningless name. 'Sunda' is not used alone, and the compound 'The Sundas' may be described as a collective singular name, proper and meaningless.

'Of the Sundas' must be taken as an adjective phrase, equivalent to 'called the Sundas.'

'With,' preposition of place, place and direction. 'With' has here its meaning of companionship, the nearest to its primary meaning.

'Its,' pronoun, demonstrative (referring to 'the group &c.'), singular number, neuter gender, possessive case. 'Its' is governed in the possessive case by the nouns following. The reference is perfectly distinct.

'Thousand,' adjective of quantity. Properly speaking, it is a definite numeral; but here it is used indefinitely, at least not with a precise meaning.

'Islands,' noun, general and significant, plural number.

'Islets,' noun, general and significant, plural number. 'Islets' is a lower class than island: it stands under 'island' with the co-ordinate class 'large islands,' thus:—

Islands.

Large islands. Islets (small islands).

'With its thousand islands and islets,' is here an adjective phrase to 'group.' It is co-ordinate, not restrictive. It is equivalent to the clause 'whose islands and islets are a thousand in number.' The idiom is peculiar. If the literal meaning of 'with' were insisted on, the group would be represented as lying beside itself. The phrase is regularly placed so as to qualify the noun it applies to.

For Analysis. SIMPLE SENTENCE.

I. *Subject,* 'group.'

II. *Attributive adjuncts of Subject*
1. 'the.'
2. 'of the Sundas,' *adjective phrase.*
3. 'with its thousand islands and islets,' *adj. phrase.*

III. *Predicate,* 'lies.'

VI. *Adverbial adjunct of Predicate* — 'to the south of Asia,' *adverbial phrase.*

5.

Triumphal arch that fill'st the sky,
When storms prepare to part!
I ask not proud philosophy
To teach me what thou art.

For Parts of Speech.—'Triumphal,' adjective of quality, restrictive, limiting the word 'arch' to a narrower class.

'Arch,' noun, general and significant; used in apposition to 'thou' (line 4) to declare its reference.

'That,' pronoun, relative, restrictive.

'Fill'st,' verb, transitive (object—'sky').

'Sky.' 'The sky' like 'the earth,' is a singular designation. When painters speak of 'a bit of sky,' they use the word as a noun of material. In the expression 'lands with brighter skies,' the word is used as a general noun, every country being supposed to have its own sky.

'When,' pronominal adverb of time, used as a conjunction.

'Storms,' noun general and significant.

'Prepare,' verb, here intransitive, usually transitive.

'Part,' verb, intransitive.

'To part,' gerundial adv. phrase of cause, qualifying 'prepare.'

'That fill'st the sky when storms prepare to part,' adjective clause, restrictive, required to specify the arch intended.

'When storms prepare to part,' adverbial clause of time.

'I,' pronoun, first personal.

'Ask,' verb, transitive (object—'to teach me what thou art'). This being one of those verbs that take what is called a secondary object, we may either suppose 'to teach &c.' to be the completion, and 'philosophy' to be the object; or we may regard 'to teach' as the object, and 'proud philosophy' as an adverbial qualification with 'from' omitted. The second seems in this case the preferable course.

'Not,' negative adverb.

'Proud,' adjective of quality, co-ordinate to 'philosophy.' 'Proud' is an epithet, not a restrictive adjunct.

'Philosophy,' noun, proper or singular, name of a branch of knowledge.

'Teach,' verb, transitive (object—'what thou art'). 'Teach,' like 'ask,' takes a secondary object, and, as in the case of 'ask,' the best way of dealing with it probably is to regard 'what thou art' as the object, and 'me' as an adverbial phrase, with the preposition 'to' omitted.

'What,' pronoun, interrogative, indefinite, complement of art.'

'Thou,' pronoun, second personal.

'Art,' verb of incomplete predication.

For Inflection.—The inflected words are 'fill'st,' 'storms,' 'prepare,' 'to part,' 'I,' 'ask,' 'to teach,' 'me,' 'thou,' 'art.'

'Fill'st,' active voice, indicative mood, present indefinite tense, singular number, second person.

'Storms,' plural number.

'Prepare,' indicative mood, present indefinite tense. [Not distinctively inflected for number or for person].

'To part,' infinitive, gerund, equivalent to 'for the purpose of parting,' or 'with a view to parting.'

'I,' singular number, common gender, nominative case.

'Ask,' active voice, indicative mood, present indefinite tense.

'To teach,' active voice, infinitive indefinite, object of transitive verb 'ask.'

'Me,' singular number, common gender, objective case.

'Thou,' singular number, common gender, nominative case.

'Art,' indicative mood, present tense, singular number, second person.

For Analysis.—COMPLEX SENTENCE.—$A + a + a\,a + a\,a\,a$.

A.

I. *Subject,* 'I.'

III. *Predicate,* 'ask not.'

IV. *Object* — 'to teach me what thou art, triumphal arch that fill'st &c.,' *infinitive with noun clause (a) as object.*

VI. *Adverbial adjunct of Predicate* — '(from) proud philosophy,' *adverbial phrase.*

a.

I. *Subject,* 'thou.'

II. *Apposition adjunct of Subject* — 'triumphal arch that fill'st the sky when storms prepare to part,' *noun with adj. and adj. clause (a a).*

III. *Predicate* { 1. *Verb of incomplete predication*, 'art.' 2. *Complement*, 'what.' }

a a.

I. *Subject*, 'that.'
III. *Predicate*, 'fill'st.'
IV. *Object*, 'the sky.'
VI. *Adverbial adjunct of Predicate* { 'when storms prepare to part,' *adv. clause (a a a).* }

a a a.

I. *Subject*, 'storms.'
III. *Predicate*, 'prepare.'
VI. *Adverbial adjuncts of Predicate* { 1. 'when,' *adverb.* 2. 'to part,' *adv. phrase.* }

6.

(1) The Jews are in every way a remarkable people. (2) Sprung from one stock, they passed the infancy of their nation in servitude among foreigners. (3) They, nevertheless, increased in numbers so rapidly that they were able to reconquer their native Palestine. (4) There they settled themselves, under a form of government and a code of laws, unlike those of any other community, rude, or civilized.

(1).

For Parts of Speech.—'The,' demonstrative adjective or definite article, limiting 'Jews.'

'Jews,' noun, common, general, or significant; a class noun. A lower class, under the higher class 'men.' They agree in being descended from Abraham, and in dwelling together as one people in Judæa. By combining the article with the noun—The Jews—we single out from among mankind the entire people called Jews.

'Are,' verb of incomplete predication.

'In,' preposition of place, rest in. Extended from signifying place to a more general meaning.

'Every,' adjective of quantity, numeral, distributive. Emphatic for 'all'—*all* ways.

'Way,' noun, common, general, and significant.

'In every way,' a phrase serving as an adverb to qualify the predicate of the sentence—'are a remarkable people.'

'A,' adjective of quantity, numeral, called the indefinite article. Singles out one remarkable people, but not any one in particular.

'Remarkable,' adjective of quality. Limits the entire class 'people' to such as are remarkable.

'A remarkable people,' completes the predicate of the sentence.

For Inflection.—Only two words in the sentence are inflected—'Jews,' and 'are.'

'Jews,' plural number of Jew: follows the general rule of forming the plural, by adding 's' to the singular.

'Are,' indicative mood, present tense, plural number, third person. The meaning of the tense is universal; the statement is true at all times.

For Analysis

I. *Subject*, 'Jews.'

II. *Adjunct of Subject*, 'the.'

III. *Predicate*
- 1. *Verb of incomplete predication*, 'are.'
- 2. *Complement*, 'a remarkable people.'

VI. *Adverbial adjunct of predicate*, 'in every way.'

For Syntax. Concord.—The *Jews are.*

Government.—No instance.

Order of words.—Regular. The subject 'the Jews,' precedes the verb 'are.' The adjectives 'the,' 'every,' 'remarkable' precede their nouns. The adverbial phrase 'in every way' is placed between the incomplete verb and its complement so as unmistakably to qualify the whole predicate.

(2)

'Sprung from one stock, they passed the infancy of their nation in servitude, among foreigners.'

For Parts of Speech and Inflection :—

'Sprung', verb, intransitive (spring), passive, perfect participle.

'From,' preposition of place, motion from (one of the case-prepositions). Lies between the participle 'sprung,' and the qualified noun, 'one stock:' having a reference to both.

'One,' adjective of quantity, numeral, definite (cardinal number). Limits 'stock' to a single definite stock.

'Stock,' noun, common, general, significant; a class noun. Limited by 'one.'

'They,' pronoun, demonstrative, plural. Refers back to 'Jews' in the previous sentence.

'Passed,' verb, transitive, active, indicative, past indefinite.

'The,' is here used to single out an attribute or quality.

'Infancy,' noun (of state), abstract, adjectival; means the same as 'being an infant.'

'Of,' preposition (one of the case prepositions), partitive meaning; used to relate or connect that part of the life of the nation called its infancy.

'Their,' adjective, pronominal, possessive, from, 'they' the plural demonstrative pronoun. Limits the class 'nation' to a single nation.

'Nation,' a noun, general, &c.

'In,' preposition of place, rest in. Passes from the meaning of 'in a place' to the more general meaning of 'in a state,' namely, 'servitude.'

Servitude,' noun, abstract, verbal. It is not derived from an adjective (like servility from servile), and so is not an adjectival abstract. It has the same meaning, as 'being in subjection.'

'In servitude,' adverbial phrase of manner or quality.

'Among,' preposition of place, place and direction. Means the same as the phrase, 'in the midst of.'

'Foreigners,' noun, general, &c., plural number.

'Among foreigners,' adverbial phrase of place. Together with the previous phrase 'in servitude' qualifies the verb 'passed, &c.'

For Analysis.

I. *Subject,* 'they.'

II. *Attributive adjunct of Subject* { 'sprung from one stock,' *participial phrase, co-ordinate.*

III. *Predicate,* 'passed.'

IV. *Object,* 'infancy.'

V. *Attributive adjuncts of Object* { 1. 'the.' 2. 'of their nation,' *adj. phrase.*

VI. *Adverbial adjuncts of Predicate* { 1. 'in servitude,' *adv. phrase.* 2. 'among foreigners,' *adv. phrase*

For Syntax. Concord.—There is here no proper concord of inflection between subject and verb. 'They' is distinctively inflected for number, but not 'passed.'

There is concord between 'they' and 'their,' both being distinctively plural.

Government.—No instance.

Order of words.—Regular. The subject 'they' precedes the verb. The verb (transitive) precedes its object—'infancy.' The pronoun 'they' has a distinct antecedent in the preceding sentence. The participial adjunct—'sprung from one stock' precedes, and is closely conjoined with 'they,' which it is in co-ordination with. If the preposition 'from' is taken with 'one stock' it makes up an adverbial phrase qualifying 'sprung,' and placed after it, according to the rule of placing adverbs with intransitive verbs.

All the adjectives precede their nouns.

All the prepositions precede their nouns.

The two adverbial phrases follow the object of the verb that they qualify; which is the general rule.

(3)

'They, nevertheless, increased in numbers so rapidly, that they were able to re-conquer their native Palestine.'

For Parts of Speech and Inflection (omitting words parsed in the foregoing examples).

'Nevertheless,' adverb; here a conjunction, co-ordinating, adversative, arrestive. Places the sentence in a kind of opposition to the foregoing.

'Increased,' verb intransitive, indicative, past indefinite.

'Numbers,' noun, general, &c., plural number. A peculiar application of the word: 'in numbers' an adverbial phrase of manner, qualifying 'increased.'

'So,' adverb of comparison; part of the co-ordinating illative conjunction 'so that.' Qualifies the adverb 'rapidly,' but by way of comparison, so as to need a farther word or clause to complete the sense.

'Rapidly,' adverb of quality (motion).

'That,' the same as 'by that,' an adverbial use of 'that.' The compound 'so that' is here a co-ordinating conjunctive phrase of consequence, or illative conjunction: it introduces the co-ordinate clause—'they were able to re-conquer,' &c.

'Were' verb of incomplete predication, indicative, past indefinite.

'All,' adjective of quality, completes the verb 'were.'

'To re-conquer,' verb, transitive, active, gerund. After verbs or adjectives of ability or fitness, the infinitive form is best regarded as a gerund.

'Native,' adjective of quality. Both 'their' and 'native' are co-ordinating and not limiting adjectives, as must be the case with a singular noun.

'Palestine,' noun (place), proper, singular, meaningless. The co-ordinating adjectives 'their,' 'native,' have the same meaning as—'Palestine, which belonged to them, and was the place of their birth.'

For Analysis.—COMPOUND SENTENCE.—A + B. [A] They nevertheless increased rapidly in numbers; [B] so that they were able to reconquer their native Palestine. A and B are united by the co-ordinating illative conjunction 'so that.'

ANALYSIS OF A.

I. *Subject*, 'they.'

III. *Predicate*, 'increased.'

VI. *Adverbial adjuncts of Predicate*	1. 'in numbers,' *adj. phrase.* 2. 'rapidly,' *adverb.* 3. 'nevertheless,' *compound adv. of Degree.*

ANALYSIS OF B.

I. *Subject*, 'they'	
III. *Predicate*	1. *Verb of incomplete predication*, 'were.' 2. *Complement*, 'able to reconquer their native Palestine,' *adj. with gerundial adv. phrase.*
VI. *Adverbial adjuncts of Predicate*	'so that,' *compound adverb of Cause.*

For Syntax.—No distinctive *Concord.* No *Government.*

Order of words.—In accordance with the general rules. The two adverbial qualifications of 'increased' follow the verb. The conjunction 'nevertheless,' which introduces the entire sentence, might be the first word of all; but this is one of the conjunctions that are sometimes placed after the first word or words of the sentence: 'however' is a common instance.

(4).

There they settled themselves, under a form of government, and a code of laws, unlike those of any other community, rude or civilized.

Parts of Speech and Inflection.—'There,' adverb of place, rest in. Substitute for a relative, or demonstrative phrase 'in that place,' the reference being to 'Palestine.'

'Settled,' verb, transitive, active, indicative, past indefinite.

'Themselves,' pronoun reflective, plural, object of 'settled.'

'Under,' preposition of place, place and direction. Relates the noun 'form' to the verb 'settled.'

'Form,' originally an abstract noun, here used with 'a' as a general noun. In the expression, 'the form of the government,' 'form' is purely abstract, indicating one aspect of the government without regard to others, such as the persons composing it. But when we say 'a form of government,' or 'forms of government,' we use either 'form,' or the entire expression 'form of government,' as a general noun.

'Of,' case-preposition, attributive meaning. Used to relate the quality 'form' to the noun 'government.' 'Government' is also an abstract noun, but it must be viewed as concrete with reference to the attribute 'form.'

'Government,' noun, abstract, active verbal.

'Code,' must be parsed like 'form;' a noun originally abstract, used as a general noun.

'Laws,' a noun general and significant.

'Unlike,' adjective of quality.

'Those,' pronoun, demonstrative, plural number. This is one of the cases where 'that' (or its plural) is undoubtedly a pronoun.

'Of,' case-preposition, partitive meaning. 'Of' has here quite a different meaning from what it has in the two preceding instances. The laws are considered a *part*, not an *attribute* of the community.

'Any,' adjective, numeral, indefinite

'Other,' adjective, numeral, distributive.

'Community,' noun, collective. Originally an adjectival a bstractnoun, meaning 'being in common.'

'Rude,' adjective of quality.

'Or,' conjunction, co-ordinating, adversative, alternative.

'Civilised,' adjective of quality. The word has the form of a perfect participle, but it is here an adjective, as we know both from its corresponding with an adjective—'rude,' and from our being at liberty to substitute for it the adjective 'civil,' which is used in Old English with the same meaning.

The whole expression—'under a form of government and a code of laws unlike those of any other community, rude or civilised,' is an adverbial phrase of place.

For Analysis.

I. *Subject,* 'they.'
III. *Predicate,* 'settled.'
IV. *Object,* 'themselves.'
VI. *Adverbial adjuncts of Predicate* { 1. 'there.'
2. 'under a form of government, and &c.,' *adverbial phrase.*

For Syntax. Concord.—The pronoun 'those' agrees in number with its antecedents 'form of government,' and 'code of laws.' The two antecedents together are plural.

Government.—'Themselves' seems to be governed in the objective case by 'settled;' but really 'themselves' is not a distinctive inflection for the objective, the pronoun has the same form for the nominative.

Order.—The only departure from the general rules is in the position of the adverb 'there:' which, for the sake of emphatic connection with its antecedent in the preceding sentence, is placed at the beginning, instead of following 'themselves.' The adjective 'unlike' follows instead of preceding its noun, because it is attended by adjuncts.

Other Works by the Author.

First English Grammar	1s. 4d.
A Higher English Grammar	2s. 6d.
English Composition and Rhetoric . . .	4s. 0d.
Illustrative English Extracts	0s. 6d.
Logic, in Two Parts—	
Deduction	4s. 0d.
Induction	6s. 6d.
Mental and Moral Science	10s. 6d.
The Senses and the Intellect	15s. 0d.
The Emotions and the Will	15s. 0d.